SHATTERED LIVES

Sexual Violence during the
Rwandan Genocide and its Aftermath

Human Rights Watch/Africa
Human Rights Watch Women's Rights Project
Fédération Internationale des Ligues des Droits de l'Homme

Human Rights Watch
New York · Washington · London · Brussels

ISBN 1-56432-208-4
Library of Congress Catalog Card Number: 96-78471

Human Rights Watch/Africa
Human Rights Watch/Africa was established in 1988 to monitor and promote the observance of internationally recognized human rights in sub-Saharan Africa. Peter Takirambudde is the executive director; Janet Fleischman is the Washington director; Suliman Ali Baldo is the senior researcher; Alex Vines is the research associate; Bronwen Manby and Binaifer Nowrojee are counsels; and Alison DesForges is a consultant. William Carmichael is the chair of the advisory committee and Alice Brown is the vice chair.

Human Rights Watch Women's Rights Project
The Human Rights Watch Women's Rights Project was established in 1990 to monitor violence against women and gender discrimination throughout the world. Dorothy Q. Thomas is the director; Regan Ralph is the Washington director; LaShawn R. Jefferson is the research associate; Robin Levi is the Orville Schell fellow; Sinsi Hernandez-Cancio is the Women's Law and Public Policy Fellow; Binaifer Nowrojee is the consultant; and Evelyn Miah and Kerry McArthur are the associates. Kathleen Peratis is chair of the advisory committee and Nahid Toubia is the vice chair.

Addresses for Human Rights Watch
485 Fifth Avenue, New York, NY 10017-6104
Tel: (212) 972-8400, Fax: (212) 972-0905, E-mail: hrwnyc@hrw.org

1522 K Street, N.W., #910, Washington, DC 20005-1202
Tel: (202) 371-6592, Fax: (202) 371-0124, E-mail: hrwdc@hrw.org

33 Islington High Street, N1 9LH London, UK
Tel: (171) 713-1995, Fax: (171) 713-1800, E-mail: hrwatchuk@gn.apc.org

15 Rue Van Campenhout, 1000 Brussels, Belgium
Tel: (2) 732-2009, Fax: (2) 732-0471, E-mail: hrwatcheu@gn.apc.org

Website Address: http://www.hrw.org
Gopher Address://gopher.humanrights.org:5000
Listserv address: To subscribe to the list, send an e-mail message to majordomo@igc.apc.org with "subscribe hrw-news" in the body of the message (leave the subject line blank).

HUMAN RIGHTS WATCH

Human Rights Watch conducts regular, systematic investigations of human rights abuses in some seventy countries around the world. Our reputation for timely, reliable disclosures has made us an essential source of information for those concerned with human rights. We address the human rights practices of governments of all political stripes, of all geopolitical alignments, and of all ethnic and religious persuasions. Human Rights Watch defends freedom of thought and expression, due process and equal protection of the law, and a vigorous civil society; we document and denounce murders, disappearances, torture, arbitrary imprisonment, discrimination, and other abuses of internationally recognized human rights. Our goal is to hold governments accountable if they transgress the rights of their people.

Human Rights Watch began in 1978 with the founding of its Helsinki division. Today, it includes five divisions covering Africa, the Americas, Asia, the Middle East, as well as the signatories of the Helsinki accords. It also includes three collaborative projects on arms transfers, children's rights, and women's rights. It maintains offices in New York, Washington, Los Angeles, London, Brussels, Moscow, Dushanbe, Rio de Janeiro, and Hong Kong. Human Rights Watch is an independent, nongovernmental organization, supported by contributions from private individuals and foundations worldwide. It accepts no government funds, directly or indirectly.

The staff includes Kenneth Roth, executive director; Cynthia Brown, program director; Holly J. Burkhalter, advocacy director; Barbara Guglielmo, finance and administration director; Robert Kimzey, publications director; Jeri Laber, special advisor; Lotte Leicht, Brussels office director; Juan Méndez, general counsel; Susan Osnos, communications director; Jemera Rone, counsel; and Joanna Weschler, United Nations representative.

The regional directors of Human Rights Watch are Peter Takirambudde, Africa; José Miguel Vivanco, Americas; Sidney Jones, Asia; Holly Cartner, Helsinki; and Eric Goldstein (acting), Middle East. The project directors are Joost R. Hiltermann, Arms Project; Lois Whitman, Children's Rights Project; and Dorothy Q. Thomas, Women's Rights Project.

The members of the board of directors are Robert L. Bernstein, chair; Adrian W. DeWind, vice chair; Roland Algrant, Lisa Anderson, William Carmichael, Dorothy Cullman, Gina Despres, Irene Diamond, Edith Everett, Jonathan Fanton, James C. Goodale, Jack Greenberg, Vartan Gregorian, Alice H. Henkin, Stephen L. Kass, Marina Pinto Kaufman, Bruce Klatsky, Harold Hongju Koh, Alexander MacGregor, Josh Mailman, Samuel K. Murumba, Andrew Nathan, Jane Olson, Peter Osnos, Kathleen Peratis, Bruce Rabb, Sigrid Rausing, Orville Schell, Sid Sheinberg, Gary G. Sick, Malcolm Smith, Domna Stanton, Nahid Toubia, Maureen White, and Rosalind C. Whitehead.

FÉDÉRATION INTERNATIONALE
DES LIGUES DES DROITS DE L'HOMME (FIDH)

The International Federation of Human Rights is an international nongovernmental organization for the defense of the human rights enshrined in the Universal Declaration of Human Rights of 1948. Created in 1922, it includes 89 national affiliates throughout the world. To date, FIDH has undertaken more than a thousand missions for investigation, observation of trials, mediation or training in some one hundred countries. FIDH enjoys consultative status with the United Nations, UNESCO, the Council of Europe and observer status with the African Commission of Human and Peoples' Rights. Patrick Baudouin is president (France). The international board is comprised of: Pascuale Bandiera (Italy), Hélène Cidade-Moura (Portugal), René Degni-Segui (the Ivory Coast), Enoch Djondang (Chad), Michael Ellman (Great Britain), Oswaldo Enriquez (Guatemala), Carmen Ferrer Peña (Spain), Cecilia Jimenez (the Philippines), Haytham Manna (Syria), Gerald McKenzie (Canada), Sabine Missistrano (Belgium), Francisco Soberon (Peru), Robert Verdier (France), vice presidents; Odile Sidem Poulain (France), Claude Katz (France) and William Bourdon (France) are secretary generals; and Philippe Vallet is treasurer. The Africa team within the executive board is composed of Catherine Choquet, deputy secretary general responsible for Africa, Eric Gillet, coordinator for Burundi and Rwanda, and Sam Wordworth, coordinator for anglophone Africa. Antoine Bernard is the executive director of FIDH, and Isabelle Plissonneau is responsible for Africa at the international secretariat.

Address for FIDH
17 Passage de la Main d'Or, Paris 75011, France
Tel: (331) 43 55 25 18, Fax: (331) 43 55 18 80,
E-mail: 106015.2023@compuserve.com

CONTENTS

ACKNOWLEDGMENTS

This report was written by Binaifer Nowrojee, a consultant to the Women's Rights Project, on the basis of interviews and research conducted in Rwanda in March and April 1996 by Binaifer Nowrojee and Janet Fleischman, Washington director of Human Rights Watch/Africa. Janet Fleischman and Alison DesForges, consultant to Human Rights Watch/Africa, contributed to the writing of the report. Substantive and logistical assistance was provided by Timothy Longman, a consultant at the time with the Rwanda office of Human Rights Watch and the Fédération Internationale des Ligues des Droits de l'Homme (FIDH). Legal research was provided by Regan Ralph, Washington director of the Women's Rights Project, Kulsum Wakabi, Women's Law and Public Policy Fellow of the Women's Rights Project and Sara Levin, consultant to Human Rights Watch. The report was edited by Dorothy Q. Thomas, Director of the Women's Rights Project and Janet Fleischman. Associate Evelyn Miah provided production assistance.

We would like to thank all the organizations and individuals interviewed for this report for their invaluable assistance. We particularly thank the rape survivors who agreed, often at great distress to themselves, to recount their experiences.

INTRODUCTION

During the 1994 genocide, Rwandan women were subjected to sexual violence on a massive scale, perpetrated by members of the infamous Hutu militia groups known as the *Interahamwe*, by other civilians, and by soldiers of the Rwandan Armed Forces (*Forces Armées Rwandaises*, FAR), including the Presidential Guard. Administrative, military and political leaders at the national and local levels, as well as heads of militia, directed or encouraged both the killings and sexual violence to further their political goal: the destruction of the Tutsi as a group. They therefore bear responsibility for these abuses.

Although the exact number of women raped will never be known, testimonies from survivors confirm that rape was extremely widespread and that thousands of women were individually raped, gang-raped, raped with objects such as sharpened sticks or gun barrels, held in sexual slavery (either collectively or through forced "marriage") or sexually mutilated. These crimes were frequently part of a pattern in which Tutsi women were raped after they had witnessed the torture and killings of their relatives and the destruction and looting of their homes. According to witnesses, many women were killed immediately after being raped.

Other women managed to survive, only to be told that they were being allowed to live so that they would "die of sadness." Often women were subjected to sexual slavery and held collectively by a militia group or were singled out by one militia man, at checkpoints or other sites where people were being maimed or slaughtered, and held for personal sexual service. The militiamen would force women to submit sexually with threats that they would be killed if they refused. These forced "marriages," as this form of sexual slavery is often called in Rwanda, lasted for anywhere from a few days to the duration of the genocide, and in some cases longer. Rapes were sometimes followed by sexual mutilation, including mutilation of the vagina and pelvic area with machetes, knives, sticks, boiling water, and in one case, acid.

Throughout the world, sexual violence is routinely directed against females during situations of armed conflict. This violence may take gender-specific forms, like sexual mutilation, forced pregnancy, rape or sexual slavery. Being female is a risk factor; women and girls are often targeted for sexual abuse on the basis of their gender, irrespective of their age, ethnicity or political affiliation.

Rape in conflict is also used as a weapon to terrorize and degrade a particular community and to achieve a specific political end. In these situations, gender intersects with other aspects of a woman's identity such as ethnicity, religion, social class or political affiliation. The humiliation, pain and terror inflicted by the rapist is meant to degrade not just the individual woman but also

1

to strip the humanity from the larger group of which she is a part. The rape of one person is translated into an assault upon the community through the emphasis placed in every culture on women's sexual virtue: the shame of the rape humiliates the family and all those associated with the survivor. Combatants who rape in war often explicitly link their acts of sexual violence to this broader social degradation. In the aftermath of such abuse, the harm done to the individual woman is often obscured or even compounded by the perceived harm to the community.

During the Rwandan genocide, rape and other forms of violence were directed primarily against Tutsi women because of both their gender and their ethnicity. The extremist propaganda which exhorted Hutu to commit the genocide specifically identified the sexuality of Tutsi women as a means through which the Tutsi community sought to infiltrate and control the Hutu community. This propaganda fueled the sexual violence perpetrated against Tutsi women as a means of dehumanizing and subjugating all Tutsi. Some Hutu women were also targeted with rape because they were affiliated with the political opposition, because they were married to Tutsi men or because they protected Tutsi. A number of women, Tutsi and Hutu, were targeted regardless of ethnicity or political affiliation. Young girls or those considered beautiful were particularly at the mercy of the militia groups, who were a law unto themselves and often raped indiscriminately.

As Rwandans begin the onerous task of rebuilding a country ravaged by bloodshed and genocide, the burden is falling heavily on Rwandan women. Rwanda has become a country of women. It is currently estimated that 70 percent of the population is female and that 50 percent of all households are headed by women. Regardless of their status—Tutsi, Hutu, displaced, returnees—all women face overwhelming problems because of the upheaval caused by the genocide, including social stigmatization, poor physical and psychological health, unwanted pregnancy and, increasingly, poverty.

In Rwanda, as elsewhere in the world, rape and other gender-based violations carry a severe social stigma. The physical and psychological injuries suffered by Rwandan rape survivors are aggravated by a sense of isolation and ostracization. Rwandan women who have been raped or who suffered sexual abuse generally do not dare reveal their experiences publicly, fearing that they will be rejected by their family and wider community and that they will never be able to reintegrate or to marry. Others fear retribution from their attacker if they speak out. Often, rape survivors suffer extreme guilt for having survived and been held for rape, rather than having been executed.

This sentiment is further reinforced by some Tutsi returnees, exiles who returned from Zaire, Burundi or Uganda after the genocide, who do not face the trauma of having survived the genocide, although they share the horror of what happened. Some of the returnees view the genocide survivors with distrust and suspicion. These survivors voice resentment against the returnees, including those in government, and criticize them for, among other issues: neglecting the problems of the genocide survivors; falsely denouncing the survivors as genocide "collaborators"; illegally appropriating the land and property of the survivors; and being politically extremist in their blanket denunciation of the Hutu. "There is always the unspoken question that is asked of survivors [by the returnees]," noted Annunciata Nyiratamba of the Association for Widows of the April Genocide (Association des veuves du genocide d'avril, AVEGA), in an interview with Human Rights Watch and the Fédération Internationale des Ligues des Droits de l'Homme (FIDH) in March. "'What did you do to survive? Who was a killer? Who was not?' Those questions are always there and it creates its own dynamic between the survivors and the returnees."

Victims of sexual abuse during the genocide suffer persistent health problems. According to Rwandan doctors, the most common problem they have encountered among raped women who have sought medical treatment has been sexually transmitted diseases, including HIV/AIDS (although it is often impossible to know if this is due to the rape). Since abortion is illegal in Rwanda, doctors have also treated women with serious complications resulting from self-induced or clandestine abortions arising from rape-related pregnancies. In a number of cases, doctors have performed reconstructive surgery for women and girls who suffered sexual mutilation at the hands of their attackers. Unfortunately the stigma surrounding sexual abuse often dissuades women from seeking the medical assistance they need.

A large number of women became pregnant as a result of rape during the genocide. Pregnancies and childbirth among extremely young girls who were raped have also posed health problems for these mothers. The "pregnancies of the war," "children of hate," "enfants non-desirés" (unwanted children) or "enfants mauvais souvenir" (children of bad memories) as they are known, are estimated by the National Population Office to be between 2,000 and 5,000. Health personnel report that some women have abandoned their children or even committed infanticide, while others have decided to keep their children. In some cases, the mother's decision to keep the child has caused deep divisions in the family, pitting those who reject the child against those who prefer to raise the child. In others, the child is being raised without problems within the community.

In addition to the social and personal trauma resulting from the injuries suffered from sexual violence, women are also facing dire economic difficulty. As a result of the genocide, many women lost the male relatives on whom they previously relied on for economic support and are now destitute. Women survivors are struggling to make ends meet, to reclaim their property, to rebuild their destroyed houses, and to raise children: their own and orphans. Some Hutu women, whose husbands were killed or are now in exile or in prison accused of genocide, are dealing with similar issues of poverty as well as with the recrimination directed at them on the basis of their ethnicity or the alleged actions of their relatives.

On top of mounting poverty, Rwandan women also face pressing problems due to their second class status under Rwandan law. Although the Rwandan constitution guarantees them full equality under the law, discriminatory practices continue to govern inheritance law, among other areas. Inheritance norms are not codified and are governed under customary law. Although there are a number of contradictory court judgments interpreting customary law, general practice has established that women cannot inherit property unless they are explicitly designated as beneficiaries. Accordingly, thousands of widows and daughters currently have no legal claim to their late husband's or father's homes, land or bank accounts because they are women. Widows whose husbands worked for state enterprises or large companies are also facing great difficulties in obtaining their husbands' pensions. A complicated application procedure, coupled with the intimidation of dealing with the authorities, has deterred many women from pursuing valid pension claims. Hutu widows who were married to Tutsi men are facing particular problems from their Tutsi in-laws who threaten them and drive them off their property. The government has initiated a legal commission to address these issues and to introduce legislation to allow women to inherit equally with men, but the reforms are expected to take a long time.

Rwandan survivors of sexual violence are particularly troubled by the lack of accountability for the abuse they suffered. They want the perpetrators of the violence against them to be held responsible. However, the Rwandan judicial system is facing systemic and profound problems that make the likelihood of justice, for both the genocide perpetrators and their victims, a remote possibility. Some 80,000 prisoners are currently held without trial in prison. Two years after the genocide, the judicial system is still not functioning. Although the lack of justice is not reserved to victims of gender-based abuse in Rwanda, it is clear that rape victims face specific obstacles, including that police inspectors documenting genocide crimes for prosecution are predominantly male and are not collecting information on rape. Many women interviewed by our team, composed solely of women, indicated that they would report rape to a female investigator, but not to a man. These problems within the law enforcement and judicial systems, coupled with the reluctance of women to come forward because of stigma and fear, greatly reduce the likelihood of rape prosecutions.

In dealing with the issues facing women, the current government must address not only the violence experienced during the genocide, but also the systematic subordination of women that has permeated most aspects of women's lives. As mentioned, the government has already initiated the process of reform of the inheritance laws, but is overwhelmed by the problems caused by the genocide, as well as by the need to change entrenched social attitudes against women. Thus reform efforts are proceeding slowly. Moreover, to date, the justice, law enforcement, health and rehabilitation ministries have no coordinated strategy to address the problems facing women. The need for such a response by the government to the situation of Rwanda's women cannot be underestimated. Without empowering Rwandan women, the overwhelming majority of the population, to rebuild their lives, the political and social transformation necessary to rebuild the country cannot succeed.

Rwandan women are also at risk of receiving little justice from the international community. In late 1994, the United Nations Security Council created the International Criminal Tribunal for Rwanda, which is tasked with bringing the organizers of the genocide to justice. An international procedure which condemns genocide and holds the perpetrators accountable will send a message that impunity for such crimes will not be tolerated by the international community. However, the International Tribunal faced serious resource constraints, and continues to confront problems of staffing and methodology. With regard to gender-based crimes in particular, these problems are magnified. Although rape constitutes a war crime and a crime against humanity, little has been done until now to effectively include gender-based violence in the Tribunal's work. The methodology and investigative procedures used heretofore by the Tribunal have not been conducive to collecting rape testimonies in the Rwandan context, and the indictments of the Tribunal to date do not include any rape charges. In July 1996, the Tribunal established a Sexual Assault Committee to coordinate the investigation of gender-based violence. At this writing, the committee has just begun to operate, with the aim of addressing strategic, legal and methodological questions confronting the investigations. We are hopeful that this initiative will lead to the implementation of more appropriate and effective procedures for gathering evidence of such crimes. If the Tribunal does not take immediate steps to address these problems and conduct effective investigations to collect the testimonies of rape victims, by the time cases are brought before the Tribunal judges it will be too late.

Although the international community shamefully stood by during the height of the genocide, foreign aid began to flow after the new government took power. The aid has focused mainly on the justice system and support for refugees and internally displaced persons (IDPs). Since July 1994, the international community has spent approximately U.S. $2.5 billion on the Rwandan refugee camps in Zaire and Tanzania, while devoting some U.S. $572 million to Rwanda itself. Within the overall aid program to Rwanda, a fairly small amount is targeted for gender-related issues, ranging from assistance for women in terms of housing, credit and income-generating activities to support for health care and trauma counseling. Despite approximately U.S. $19 million going to the Rwandan judiciary, there are currently no programs designed to enhance the capacity of Rwandan police or police inspectors to investigate gender-related crimes, including rape and sexual violence during the genocide and current abuses against women. Some assistance is being provided for reform of discriminatory aspects of the legal code, including inheritance and succession laws, although much more is needed in order to move that process forward. Programs are also targeting vulnerable groups, including widows.

In addition to the Tribunal and various humanitarian efforts, the U.N. has also established the Human Rights Field Operation in Rwanda, which has a mandate to protect and promote human rights and to investigate the human rights situation in Rwanda, including investigating violations of human rights and humanitarian law, monitoring the ongoing human rights situation, and implementing programs of technical cooperation, especially in the area of the administration of justice. The Human Rights Operation also brings deficiencies in the judicial and law enforcement systems to the attention of the government. At the moment, however, the Human Rights Operation has no thematic focus to address current human rights problems facing women.

Research for this report was conducted by Human Rights Watch/FIDH in March and April 1996. The names of all the rape survivors interviewed have been changed to protect their privacy and safety. Human Rights Watch/FIDH worked closely with Rwandan women's organizations and other nongovernmental organizations in order to approach rape survivors through individuals whom they trusted. When interpretation was necessary, we used Rwandan women interpreters, usually genocide survivors themselves. In all interviews, we strove to provide women with the time and privacy required for them to relate their experiences. In addition to interviewing women victims/survivors of rape in six of the eleven prefectures, Human Rights Watch/FIDH met with a wide array of nongovernmental human rights and women's rights organizations, social workers, journalists, doctors and nurses. Within the Rwandan government, we met with representatives of the Ministry of Family and the Promotion of Women, the Ministry of Justice, the Ministry of Health and the prosecutor's office. We also met with representatives from a number of international humanitarian organizations as well as the United

Nations Human Rights Operation, the UNAMIR peacekeeping operation and the International Criminal Tribunal for Rwanda.

The future of Rwanda is largely in the hands of its women. With a population that is 70 percent female, it will be the women who will rebuild the country. Many of these women have lived through unimaginable suffering at the hands of those who carried out the genocide. Many have lost everything they had. Despite the overwhelming odds facing them, Rwandan women have begun to organize themselves and to rebuild their shattered lives. However, their efforts are greatly limited by the inattention of the Rwandan government and the international community to the past and present problems facing women, the subsequent lack of services designed to assist women, and the traditional and institutional constraints placed on women. For these reasons, it is imperative that the international community and the Rwandan government address in a sustained and effective manner the current problems and critical needs facing the majority of the population.

RECOMMENDATIONS

To the Rwandan Government

- The sexual violence that took place during the genocide should be fully investigated and where possible, prosecuted and punished. The Ministry of Justice should ensure that all police inspectors receive mandatory training on the issue of rape and other sexual abuse, including their status as crimes punishable by law. Specifically, we urge that police inspectors investigating genocide crimes receive training to ensure that discriminatory attitudes about female victims of sexual abuse do not prevent serious investigation of sexual abuse or undermine its effective prosecution. A greater number of female police inspectors should be hired and trained in order to collect rape testimonies in a more systematic and effective manner.

- The effectiveness of the law depends on cooperation and coordination among different government ministries. An inter-ministerial task force should be created to deal with the violence inflicted on women during the genocide and related current problems facing women, with the aim of improving the social, medical and legal responses to women's needs in the aftermath of genocide. This body should meet on a regular basis in order to improve and coordinate the government's delivery of services to women. It should include, at a minimum, representatives from the Ministries of Women and the Family, Justice, Health and Rehabilitation as well as from the nongovernmental women's organizations.

- While Human Rights Watch and FIDH are encouraged by the Rwandan government's efforts to revise the discriminatory aspects of Rwandan law, we urge the government to enact the revisions expeditiously. In the interim, the government must take immediate steps to ensure that women are not arbitrarily driven off their property. Moreover, the government must ensure that once the laws are revised, programs are put into place to implement the new laws and to remedy the effects of discrimination.

- The Ministry of Health should make every effort to address health issues for women resulting from the genocide. Appropriate medical care, including basic gynecological treatment, should be provided to women and girls.

- The government should ensure that international relief and aid projects that assist women are coordinated and implemented throughout the

8

country to ensure that such services are equally available to women in each prefecture.

To the International Criminal Tribunal for Rwanda

- The International Tribunal must fully and fairly investigate and prosecute sexual violence. Rape, sexual slavery and sexual mutilation should be recognized and prosecuted, where appropriate, as crimes against humanity, genocide crimes, or war crimes.

- The International Tribunal must step up its efforts to integrate a gender perspective into its investigations. Previous investigative methodology and procedures, which have failed to elicit rape testimonies, must be amended. In particular, the Tribunal must ensure that the issue of violence against women is treated with the same gravity as other crimes against humanity within its jurisdiction. Investigations of rape and other forms of sexual assault should be conducted by teams that include women investigators and interpreters (preferably women) skilled in interviewing women survivors of gender-based violence in the larger context of the atrocities which occurred. Rape survivors should be given the requisite privacy and time to relate the crimes committed against them to Tribunal investigators. The investigators should also explain to interviewees the basic procedures of the investigation.

- Existing indictments should be amended, where appropriate, to ensure that rape, sexual slavery and sexual mutilation charges are brought. If need be, further investigation should be conducted by the Tribunal investigators to collect information on sexual violence previously overlooked.

- The Witness Protection Unit must be strengthened and expanded. Protection programs should be designed to protect the victim and witnesses against potential reprisals and be capable of responding to various protection needs. Support services must also be provided to victims and witnesses, including legal counseling to prepare them for giving testimony; trauma counseling, especially for those who suffered sexual abuse; medical attention; transport for family or other victims to accompany victims or witnesses to Arusha; and relocation of victims, witnesses, and their families, if they so desire. The prosecutor's office must also have discretionary funds to provide for emergency protection, including relocation. Given the difficulties in protecting people in such a small and interconnected country, the victims and witnesses should be invited to suggest measures that they believe would increase their security. The Witness Protection Unit should monitor the safety of victims and witnesses on a regular basis. For those victims and witnesses who are outside of Rwanda, the Tribunal must coordinate with the relevant national government to ensure the individual's protection.

To the United Nations Human Rights Field Operation in Rwanda
- The United Nations Human Rights Field Operation in Rwanda should ensure that its monitoring of human rights abuses includes reporting on current incidents of rape and sexual assault against women involving state agents and that such offenses are appropriately denounced. Human Rights Operation Field Officers should receive training to ensure that discriminatory attitudes about female rape victims do not prevent serious investigation of rape or sexual abuse. Reports of sexual violence should be collected in a more systematic manner, keeping in mind the need for privacy and sensitivity in order to obtain testimony from rape victims.

- The Human Rights Field Operation in Rwanda should apply its monitoring and advisory role with regard to the Rwandan judicial system to ensuring the well-being of women (and their children) who require assistance in order to enjoy the equal protection of the law, especially in the area of inheritance and property rights. Although the Rwandan government has initiated a legal reform project to review such laws, the Human Rights Field Operation should call on the government to take interim steps to address the pressing problems facing women who are driven off their property and to monitor the progress of the legal reform.

To International Donors (the United Nations, the United States, the European Union, the Netherlands, Belgium, Germany, and others), and Humanitarian Organizations
- International donors and humanitarian organizations should ensure that their programs in Rwanda address women's needs, especially in the areas of criminal justice, health care, housing, credit, education, vocational training, and trauma counseling. To the degree possible, programs for rape survivors should be integrated into broader programs to ensure that rape survivors are not further stigmatized.

- International donors should provide support for training judicial and law enforcement personnel—particularly investigators of genocide crimes—on gender-based crimes against women. Programs should also be devised that would enhance the recruitment of women investigators.

- Financial and logistical support must be assured for the International Tribunal and for the United Nations Human Rights Field Operation. Targeted funding should be provided to ensure that the International Tribunal and the Human Rights Field Operation improve their investigation of gender-based abuses. In particular, funding should be provided to the International Tribunal for experienced female investigators trained in working with victims of gender-based crimes.

BACKGROUND

The Genocide

During the months of April to July 1994, between 500,000 and one million Rwandan men, women and children were slaughtered in a genocide of the Tutsi minority and in massacres of moderate Hutu who were willing to work with Tutsi. A circle of political leaders, threatened with the loss of political power, organized the killings with the help of the military, Hutu militiamen and many other civilians.[1]

President Juvenal Habyarimana and a close circle of supporters had governed since 1973, when Habyarimana had taken power in a coup. Himself a Hutu, Habyarimana was initially popular with the majority Hutu, generally estimated to have been some 85 percent of the population. But by the end of the 1980s, the ruling group was losing support, partly because of corruption and increasing repression, partly because of general economic decline. Under pressure from a growing internal opposition and from international donors, Habyarimana was facing the end of his personal monopoly of power and of the exclusive control of his party, the National Republican Democratic Movement (*Mouvement National Républicain Democratique*, MRND). At the same time, his regime was also threatened by an invasion of Rwanda by the Rwandan Patriotic Front (RPF), a group based in Uganda and made up mostly of Tutsi refugees. Tutsi had ruled Rwanda before and during the colonial era, but were driven from power by a revolution beginning in 1959 that killed some 20,000 Tutsi and drove tens of thousands more into exile. In the face of continued refusal to permit their return, the refugees had organized an effective army to cross the border and unseat the regime.

Habyarimana and his followers hoped to use the 1990 RPF attack to rebuild their slipping base of power by rallying the majority Hutu against the Tutsi. They began a campaign to label all Tutsi and Hutu allied with them as "accomplices" of the invaders. The government arrested some 8,000 Tutsi and Hutu opposed to the government immediately after the invasion. Two weeks later, local government officials directed a massacre of Tutsi, the first in a series of killings that would set the pattern for the genocide of 1994. By 1993 Habyarimana and his circle had put in place all the elements needed for the genocide: a propaganda machine that operated first through the written press and national radio

---

[1]See Human Rights Watch, *Slaughter Among Neighbors: The Political Origins of Communal Violence* (New Haven: Human Rights Watch/Yale University Press, 1995), pp. 3, 13-32.

and later through a supposedly private radio station, *Radio Télévision Libre des Mille Collines* (RTLM), that in fact benefited from official support; an organization of militia groups recruited largely from unemployed young men and trained to kill; supplies of arms and ammunition that had been distributed clandestinely; and a network of committed administrators, military, and political leaders ready to lead the attack.

The international community ignored both the smaller massacres between 1990 and 1993 and the preparations for the catastrophic genocide. It focused instead on bringing about an end to the war between the Rwandan government and the RPF, a goal apparently achieved in August 1993 with the signing of the Arusha Accords. As stipulated in the agreement, the United Nations provided a peace-keeping force (United Nations Assistance Mission in Rwanda, UNAMIR) to facilitate the transition to an elected government and to oversee the integration of the Rwandan Armed Forces with the RPF army. But the U.N. wanted a cheap success and failed to provide either the mandate needed or the forces necessary to ensure a prompt and orderly transition. Determined to prevent implementation of the agreement which he had signed, Habyarimana created one obstacle after another to the installation of the transitional government, playing skillfully upon divisions within the internal opposition which was to share power with the Habyarimana group and with the RPF in the new government. The RPF refused the changes requested by Habyarimana and the process dragged on from August 1993 to April 1994. During that period, both sides prepared to resume war. The extremists around Habyarimana pushed forward their plans for the genocide, which they apparently saw as a weapon for simultaneously winning the war against the RPF and recapturing leadership of the political scene within Rwanda.

On April 6, 1994, Habyarimana's plane was shot down as he was returning from a peace conference in Tanzania. People close to Habyarimana, including those at Radio RTLM, immediately blamed the RPF for his death but offered no convincing proof of this guilt. The identity of those responsible for downing the plane has never been determined. The killing of Habyarimana served as a pretext to initiate the massive killings that had been planned for months, both of Tutsi and of those Hutu who were opposed to Habyarimana. In addition, Rwandan army soldiers killed ten Belgian soldiers who were part of UNAMIR, after they had been told that Belgium had helped the RPF shoot down the plane. The extremists had spread this false information to ensure an attack on the Belgians, whom they wanted out of Rwanda because they were the best trained and the best equipped of the UNAMIR force. Five days after the genocide began, Belgium did withdraw its own troops and began exerting pressure on other members of the Security Council to remove all of the peace-keeping force. On

April 21, the Security Council decided to pull out all but several hundred of the soldiers who were then protecting some 20,000 persons at risk, many of them Tutsi.

Confident that the international community would not intervene, the organizers of the genocide extended and intensified the killing after the departure of most of the UNAMIR forces. Following lines laid out by national political, administrative and military leaders, local level authorities and politicians led the effort to extirpate the Tutsi and moderate Hutu. Often they worked together with soldiers or national policemen (officially part of the Rwandan Armed Forces) to launch the killing. Organized militia often operated under the orders of both civilian and military officials, as well as following the directives of the heads of the parties with which they were affiliated. Ordinary citizens, although untrained and not specifically organized to kill, also joined in attacks on Tutsi and moderate Hutu, following the lead of militia or other authorities. Many of these ordinary citizens acted from fear, both fear of the Tutsi whom they had been taught were coming to kill them, and fear of other Hutu who threatened reprisals on any who did not join in the carnage.

Once the genocide began, the RPF renewed its military offensive against the government. Horrified by the extent of the killing and by the costs of supporting the refugees who flooding across the border at the end of April, the U.N. decided on May 17 to send an expanded peace-keeping force, UNAMIR II, to Rwanda. Because of bureaucratic delays at the U.N. and lack of political will among potential donor nations, the new force did not begin to arrive until August. By that time, the RPF had defeated the genocidal government and had established a new government.[2]

The defeated government and army, fearing retribution for their crimes, led a mass exodus of some two million Hutu into neighboring countries. The ensuing refugee crisis, unprecedented in its scale and the speed with which it occurred, resulted in the death of some 50,000 predominantly Hutu refugees from disease, hunger, and lack of water in neighboring Zaire and Tanzania.

Hundreds of thousands of Hutu, both genocide perpetrators and others, remain in refugee camps in Zaire and Tanzania, fearful of arrest and prosecution if they return. The perpetrators of the genocide continue to organize military offensives over the Rwanda-Zaire border and pose a security threat to the current Rwandan government. Within the refugee camps, those who organized the

---

[2]When the RPF launched its military offensive to end the genocide and take over the country, there were accusations of RPF abuses against Hutu civilians. However, rape was not widely reported. This has been attributed to the presence of women RPF fighters in the ranks, and because of the strict discipline enforced by the RPF leadership at that time.

genocide also use terror and violence against the refugees, some of whom followed them only reluctantly into exile. Some of these refugees have been prevented from returning to Rwanda. Within Rwanda, the country remains polarized with continuing distrust and tension between the two ethnic groups and growing repression against the civilian population by the current government.[3]

The Rwandan government must also deal with the complex problems of reintegrating nearly one million Tutsi who had been living in exile and who have returned to Rwanda since 1994. Following the end of the genocide and the RPF take-over, large numbers of these Tutsi exiles flocked to Rwanda, particularly from Uganda, Burundi and Zaire. For some returnees, it was their first time in Rwanda, since they were born as refugees in neighboring countries, or fled when they were young children. Many serve in the current government or in the military. Although the returnees are not facing the trauma of having survived the genocide, they too share the horror of their compatriots and some are facing economic problems similar to those of the survivors. Many returnees occupied abandoned or deserted property on their arrival in the country. As survivors of the genocide, Tutsi returning from exile, and Hutu refugees coming home have sought to reoccupy their property, many and complex disputes over housing and property have arisen. The government has not yet come to terms with these enormous problems.

Genocide Propaganda Against Tutsi Women

In the years preceding the genocide, the organizers used propaganda to heighten fear and hatred between Hutu and Tutsi. Through the written press and then through the RTLM radio, extremists taught that the two were different peoples: the Hutu, part of the larger category of "Bantu" and the Tutsi, part of the "Ethiopid" or "Nilotic" group. Such categories, once thought to be real, are now recognized to be inaccurate groupings, a legacy of nineteenth century European racism. Simplifying and distorting history, the propagandists insisted that Tutsi were foreign conquerors who had mastered the majority Hutu through a combination of ruse and ruthlessness. According to these beliefs, the Tutsi had

---

[3]See also, Human Rights Watch/FIDH, "Rwanda: The Crisis Continues,"*a Human Rights Watch short report*, Vol. 7, No. 1, April 1995; Human Rights Watch/FIDH press release "New Attacks on Judicial Personnel in Rwanda," May 13, 1996; Human Rights Watch/FIDH press release "Human Rights Watch and the International Federation of Human Rights Leagues Condemn New Killings in Rwanda," July 26, 1996; Human Rights Watch, *Human Rights Watch World Report 1996*, (New York: Human Rights Watch, 1995), pp. 40-47.

refused to accept the destruction of their power through the 1959 revolution and were determined to reassert control over the Hutu.

In their drive to dominate, propagandists said, Tutsi used their women—thought to be more beautiful than Hutu women—to infiltrate Hutu ranks. "Tutsi women have always been viewed as enemies of the state," said one Tutsi woman:

> No military man could marry Tutsi women, or they would have to leave the military. Tutsi women were considered more beautiful, which bred hate against them. The Kinyarwanda word used was *Ibizungerezi* about Tutsi women [which means beautiful and sexy]. It led to jealously, to a hate that I can't describe . . . I was told that I couldn't work in certain places because as a Tutsi women I would poison the others.[4]

"The propaganda warned Hutu men to beware of Tutsi women," explained one Tutsi woman. "For example, it said if she gives you a good child, the child is not really for you—the child is really for her Tutsi brothers. 'These women are very sexual, and they sleep with their Tutsi brothers. You will be deceived by them.'"[5] The stereotypes also portrayed Tutsi women as being arrogant and looking down on Hutu men whom they considered ugly and inferior.

Beginning in 1990, over a dozen newspapers in Kinyarwanda or French were launched that systematically exploited ethnic hatred.[6] Although they had a relatively small circulation, mostly in the capital Kigali, these papers were often taken to the countryside by urban workers on the weekends and their message was shared widely in rural communities. In some cases, the local authorities in the rural areas were provided with copies of these publications. In addition to articles

---

[4]Human Rights Watch/FIDH interview, member, *Association des femmes chefs de familles*, Kigali, March 28, 1996. Many Rwandans believe that Hutu soldiers were prohibited from marrying Tutsi women. This appears to have been an unwritten rule rather than any official regulation. In fact, a number of military officers did have Tutsi wives at the time of the genocide, so the rule, if it existed, was either implemented after these marriages had taken place or was not rigorously enforced.

[5]Human Rights Watch/FIDH interview, Kigali, March 25, 1996.

[6]Jean-Pierre Chrétien, *Rwanda: Les Médias du génocide* (Paris: Karthala and Reporters sans frontières, 1995 ed.), pp. 45-47.

excoriating the Tutsi community, the magazines printed graphic cartoons to portray Tutsi women using their supposed sexual prowess on U.N. peacekeepers (RPF supporters according to the propaganda) and the moderate Prime Minister Agathe Uwilingiyimana in various sexual poses with other politicians.[7]

Kangura ("Wake Up" in Kinyarwanda), a predecessor to the RTLM radio station, was the first and most virulent voice of hate. Although it had a relatively small circulation of approximately 10,000, *Kangura* was distributed to the local burgomasters and was actively supported by powerful government and military patrons.[8] Because of these links, *Kangura* was able to obtain important information and to publish accurate political predictions, which gave the paper credibility. In one issue, it foretold the death of President Habyarimana.[9]

Kangura often warned the Hutu to be on guard against Tutsi women. According to *Kangura*, "[t]he *Inkotanyi*," (a word used to refer to the RPF meaning "fierce fighter" in Kinyarwanda), "will not hesitate to transform their sisters, wives and mothers into pistols" to conquer Rwanda.[10] In the December 1990 issue of *Kangura*, journalist Hassan Ngeze published "The Ten Commandments of the Hutu," four of which dealt specifically with women:

> Every Hutu should know that a Tutsi woman, wherever she is, works for the interest of her Tutsi ethnic group. As a result, we shall consider a traitor any Hutu who: marries a Tutsi woman; befriends a Tutsi woman; employs a Tutsi woman as a secretary or a concubine.

> Every Hutu should know that our Hutu daughters are more suitable and conscientious in their role as woman, wife and mother of the family. Are they not beautiful, good secretaries and more honest?

---

[7]Ibid., pp. 336, 368.

[8]Ibid., p. 32.

[9]African Rights, *Rwanda: Death, Despair and Defiance*, rev. ed. (London: African Rights, 1995), pp. 74-75.

[10]*Kangura*, issue number 19, July 1991 as quoted in Chrétien, *Rwanda: Les Médias du génocide*, p. 161.

Hutu woman, be vigilant and try to bring your husbands, brothers and sons back to reason.

The Rwandese Armed Forces should be exclusively Hutu. The experience of the October [1990] war has taught us a lesson. No member of the military shall marry a Tutsi.[11]

Another issue of *Kangura* accused Tutsi women of monopolizing positions of employment in both the public and private sectors, hiring their Tutsi sisters on the basis of their thin noses (a stereotypically "Tutsi feature"), thereby contributing to the unemployment rate of the Hutu, particularly Hutu women.[12]

Kangura called on Hutu to use the necessary vigilance against the Tutsi (which it dubbed the *inyenzi*: cockroaches) and accomplice Hutu (*ibyitso*: traitors). One Hutu woman commented, "according to the propaganda, the Tutsi were hiding the enemy. And their beautiful women were being used to do it. So, everybody knew what that meant."[13]

When the violence began in 1994, rape of Tutsi women was widespread. The targeted use of sexual violence against Tutsi women was fueled by both ethnic and gender stereotypes; Tutsi women were targeted on the basis of the genocide propaganda which had portrayed them as calculated seductress-spies bent on dominating and undermining the Hutu. Tutsi women were also targeted because of the gender stereotype which portrayed them as beautiful and desirable, but inaccessible to Hutu men whom they allegedly looked down upon and were "too good" for. Rape served to shatter these images by humiliating, degrading, and ultimately destroying the Tutsi woman. Even Tutsi women married to Hutu men were not spared, despite the custom that a wife was protected by her husband's lineage after marriage. Most of the women interviewed described how their rapists mentioned their ethnicity before or during the rape. Rape survivors recounted comments such as: "We want to see how sweet Tutsi women are;" or "You Tutsi women think that you are too good for us;" or "We want to see if a Tutsi woman is like a Hutu woman;" or "If there were peace, you would never accept me." When asked why rape was so widespread, one Rwandan woman who works with

---

[11]*Kangura*, issue number 6, December 1990 as quoted in African Rights, *Rwanda: Death, Despair and Defiance*, pp.42-43.

[12]*Kangura*, issue number 29, January 1992, pp.16-17 as quoted in Ibid., p. 146.

[13]Human Rights Watch/FIDH interview, Kigali, March 18, 1996.

a nongovernmental organization in Kigali said, "Hutu men wanted to know Tutsi women, to have sex with them. Tutsi women were supposed to be special sexually.[14] Other women noted that their attackers said, "You Tutsi girls are too proud," apparently setting the stage for their degradation.

The propaganda fueled the ethnic and gender stereotypes, leading people to believe that "Hutu women were made for work, to be servants," as a journalist explained. She continued:

> Tutsi women were made for sexuality and beauty, for royal courts. That's how we were educated. People from the north, where there were few Tutsi, wanted to take Tutsi as mistresses because they were forbidden to have them. Tutsi women were seen as spies because they know how to present themselves to whites and to Hutu men, so they became an arm of the RPF. Hutu understood the propaganda. It was time for revenge . . .[15]

The Status of Women in Rwandan Society

In a post-genocide Rwanda, where women are estimated to make up some 70 percent of the population, women's subordinate status in society has far-reaching implications. Although Article 16 of the 1991 Rwandan Constitution guarantees equality, women have long been subjected to a wide array of limitations and restrictions which have discriminated against them in profound and systemic ways.

Within Rwandan society, women have traditionally been regarded and treated as dependents of their male relatives. Throughout their lives, women are expected to be managed and protected by their fathers, their husbands and their male children. Traditionally, the role of a Rwandan woman in society has centered around her position as wife and mother. Hagaruka, a legal aid organization based in Kigali, which provides representation to women, noted in one of its publications on the rights of women in the family that:

> From a young age, the education that girls receive from their mothers initiates them into their future lives as wives and mothers. A woman will take care of the house as well as

---

[14]Human Rights Watch/FIDH interview, member, *Association des femmes chefs de familles*, Kigali, March 28, 1996.

[15]Human Rights Watch/FIDH interview, Kigali, March 19, 1996.

working in the fields. She will learn certain kinds of behavior, such as keeping a reserved attitude, or submission . . . The strength of a family is measured in the number of its boys.[16]

Women's ability to seek opportunities beyond the home have been greatly limited by the idealized image of women as child-bearers. Women are most valued for the number of children they can produce, and prior to the genocide, the average number of children per woman (6.2) was one of the highest rates in the world.[17]

According to a 1995 government report prepared for the United Nations Fourth World Conference on Women:

> The ideal image of a woman is still generally viewed through the perspective of her maternal role. The woman must be fertile, hard-working, and reserved. She must learn the art of silence and reserve.[18]

The stereotypical woman is expected to be docile, and domestic abuse is common. The Rwandan government report estimates that one-fifth of Rwandan women are victims of domestic violence at the hands of their male partners.[19] One Rwandan proverb states that a woman who is not yet battered is not a real woman.

According to the 1995 government report, the patriarchal structure of Rwandan society denied women access to opportunities outside the home, and has historically discriminated against women, both formally and informally, in education, health, politics and employment. The traditional and legal constraints placed on women by society have been compounded by a lack of knowledge on the part of women themselves about their rights and a lack of power to enforce them. High levels of poverty generally contributed further to the secondary status of women. Before the genocide, Rwanda was classified among the twenty-five

------

[16]Charles Ntampaka, *La Femme et la Fille dans leur Famille d'Origine*, (Kigali: Hagaruka [*Association pour la défense des droits de la Femme et de l'Enfant*]/United States Embassy, 1993), pp. 24-25.

[17]This figure was applicable in 1992. Ibid., p. 13, 54.

[18]Government of Rwanda, *Rapport National du Rwanda pour la Quatrième Conference Mondiale sur les Femmes (Beijing)*, September 1995, p. 19.

[19]Ibid., p. 70.

poorest nations in the world, with 94 percent of its population engaged in subsistence agriculture. At that time, women constituted 51.3 percent of the population.[20]

Prior to the genocide, women were significantly under-represented in education and politics. In the 1980s, girls represented some 45 percent of students in primary school. Among secondary school students, boys outnumbered girls 9 to 1, and by university level, men outnumbered women by 15 to 1. Most women remain in the home from puberty onwards. When faced with financial difficulties, parents were more inclined to remove their girl children rather than their boys from school. Not surprisingly, levels of illiteracy among women are extremely high.[21]

During the 1980s, maternal mortality was the major health problem facing women. Eighty percent of pregnant women delivered their children at home. Sixty-three percent of deaths among women in 1993 were related to their reproductive system.[22] Insufficient maternal health care, a lack of family planning facilities, and a lack of medical technology all combined to deny women adequate pre- and post-natal care. Malnutrition among women was also very high.[23]

Within political life, the Constitution guarantees the right of all citizens to participate in politics without distinction based on sex or other enumerated grounds. However, few women participated in political life prior to the genocide. As voters, women's choices were often imposed on them by their husbands.[24] As politicians, women's participation was extremely low prior to the genocide. In parliament, women's participation never rose above 17 percent. Within the executive branch of government, there were no women appointees until 1990, when women constituted a mere 5.26 percent. There were no women in ministerial positions until 1990. Three women served as ministers in the multi-party governments established after 1991. One, Agathe Uwilingiyimana, took office as prime minister in July 1993. Known to be a moderate who would have opposed the genocide, she was one of the first national leaders killed when the carnage was launched. In 1992, the government created the Ministry of Family and the

---

[20]Ibid., p. 13.

[21]Ibid., pp. 19-20.

[22]Ibid., p. 53.

[23]Ibid., p. 20.

[24]Ntampaka, *La Femme et la Fille dans la Societé*, p. 6.

Promotion of Women.   Within local government, there were no female burgomasters or prefects before the genocide, and only 3.2 percent of sub-prefects were women.

Although women constituted over half the economically active population in the years leading up to the genocide, they rarely benefited from their labor because of discriminatory laws which denied them land ownership and informal discrimination which limited their ability to obtain credit. Most Rwandan women, at the time of the genocide, were based in the agricultural sector as subsistence farmers working on the family plot of land. An estimated 65-70 percent of agricultural work was done by women.[25] A 1991 study found that women took greater responsibility than men for land cultivation and water collection in addition to being responsible for the children and the household. Yet, they were not remunerated for their contribution, nor were they eligible for credit or loans. Women were often required to obtain their husband's authorization in order to qualify for credit. The division of labor in this manner had the effect of permitting men to work in salaried occupations and commercial operations in the private sector, further marginalizing women from this sector.[26] Moreover, the Commercial Code contains a provision stipulating that a wife cannot engage in commercial activity or employment without the express authorization of her husband.[27]

Prior to the genocide, the private sector in Rwanda was extremely small, with private enterprises employing only about 10 percent of the population. Between 1986 to 1990, women made up only 12.21-18.65 percent of this small sector of the work force. At that time, no more than 5 percent of company directors were women. Prejudice against the ability of women is cited by the current government as the main reason for this low number. Women were represented in greater numbers at the lower levels of the private sector, but again, that number was still very low: Of 8,441 private enterprises, only 1,162 (13.76 percent) even hired women. The Employment Code prohibits the employment of

---

[25]Government of Rwanda, *Rapport National*, p. 37.

[26]Réseau des femmes oeuvrant pour le development rural. *Profil socio-economique de la femme rwandaise*, Kigali, May 1991, p. 47.

[27]Article 4, Des Commercants et de la Preuve des Engagement Commerciaux (1925) as quoted in Delphine Tailfer, *Recueil de Textes sur les Droits de la Femme*, (Kigali: Projet de Révision Légale, Ministère de la Famille et de la Promotion de la Femme/UNICEF, 1995), p. 50.

women in any job that requires her to work at night.[28] In the public sector, women were represented in greater number and constituted almost 40 percent of workers; however, they were concentrated predominantly at the administrative levels or in traditionally lower paying occupations, such as teaching, social work or nursing.[29]

The profound discrimination against women has carried over into a post-genocide Rwanda and poses serious problems for women, particularly given that they now constitute roughly 70 percent of the population. Many survivors are widows who lost their families in the genocide and found themselves displaced or refugees with no remaining male relatives. Others are women whose husbands fled the country when the RPF-led government took over. Still others are young girls whose families were killed or have fled the country. Many households are headed by women who are in turn supporting children—their own, children of relatives, and orphans they have taken in. Their subordinate status continues to disadvantage them as they attempt to rebuild their lives.

As a result of the past and current discrimination, many female genocide survivors have been reduced to an even lower standard of living now that they are widowed or orphaned. Most female genocide survivors have little education, lack marketable skills, and are often denied access to their husband's or father's property because they are women. In a 1995 survey conducted of 304 rape survivors by the Ministry of Family and Promotion of Women in collaboration with UNICEF, the women were all living in difficult circumstances. Thirty-two percent were living alone without any surviving family. Barely any of the women were educated beyond primary school, 61.8 percent had completed primary school, 25.7 percent had completed secondary school, and 10 percent had never attended school. Forty-one percent of the women were working in subsistence farming, 34 percent were students; and 19 percent were state or private sector employees.[30] In addition, rates of maternal and infant mortality as well as malnutrition have reportedly risen since the genocide.[31]

---

[28]Ntampaka, *La Femme et la Fille dans la Societé*, p. 12, citing (Article 121 of the Employment Code).

[29]Government of Rwanda, *Rapport National*, pp. 14-23.

[30]Ministry of Family and the Promotion of Women, "Enquête effectuee aupres des victimes" March-April 1995.

[31]Government of Rwanda, *Rapport National*, p. 43.

PROBLEMS DOCUMENTING GENDER-BASED CRIMES

Although exact figures will never be known, testimonies from survivors confirm that rape was extremely widespread. Some observers believe that almost every woman and adolescent girl who survived the genocide was raped.[32] While the ages of women and girls raped ranged from as young as two years old to over fifty, most rapes were perpetrated against young women between the ages of sixteen and twenty-six. The survey of 304 rape survivors conducted by the Ministry of Family and Promotion of Women in collaboration with UNICEF found their average age to be twenty-four years old. Among them, 28 percent were under eighteen years; 43.75 percent were between nineteen and twenty-six; 17.1 percent were between twenty-seven and thirty five; 8.55 percent were between thirty-six and forty-five; and 1.6 percent were over forty-five; 0.7 percent did not respond. Among the group, 63.8 percent were young single women.[33]

The only attempts to estimate the overall level of gender-based violence against women have been through extrapolations based on the numbers of recorded pregnancies as a result of rape. In a January 1996 report, the United Nations Special Rapporteur on Rwanda, Rene Degni-Segui, found that:

> rape was the rule and its absence the exception . . . According to the statistics, one hundred cases of rape give rise to one pregnancy. If this principle is applied to the lowest figure [the numbers of pregnancies caused by rape are estimated to be between 2,000-5,000], it gives at least 250,000 cases of rape and the highest figure would give 500,000, although this figure also seems excessive. However, the important aspect is not so much the number as the principle and the types of rape.[34]

---

[32]Catherine Bonnet, "Le viol des femmes survivantes du génocide du Rwanda," in *Rwanda: Un génocide du XXe siècle*, Raymond Verdier, Emmanuel Decaux, Jean-Pierre Chrétien eds., (Paris: Editions L'Harmattan, 1995), p. 18.

[33]Ministry of Family and the Promotion of Women, "Enquête effectuee aupres des victimes."

[34]United Nations, *Report on the Situation of Human Rights in Rwanda submitted by Mr. René Degni-Segui, Special Rapporteur of the Commission on Human Rights*, under paragraph 20 of the resolution S-3/1 of 25 May 1994, E/CN.4/1996/68, January 29, 1996, p. 7.

Doctors have also confirmed the high numbers of rape victims they examined immediately after the genocide. Dr. Odette Nyiramilimo of Le Bon Samaritain Clinic in Kigali estimated that immediately following the genocide, two rape cases a day were coming into the clinic. Most had vaginal infections and some tested positive for HIV (although it was impossible to tell if they had contracted the infection as a result of rape).[35]

The difficulty of accurately documenting the occurrence of sexual violence during the Rwandan genocide is due to a number of factors. Worldwide, victims of rape are stigmatized and made to feel shame for the crime committed against them. As a result, rape is one of the most under-reported crimes. As elsewhere, rape victims in Rwanda have been reluctant to disclose publicly that they have been raped in part because they fear rejection and shame, however undeserved, for themselves and their families. One rape survivor said "after rape, you don't have value in the community."[36]

The difficulty of collecting information on rape is compounded by fear. Rwandan women are reticent to talk because some of the perpetrators are still living among them. They know who killed their families and raped them. "Women here are scared to talk because it was their neighbors who raped them," Bernadette Muhimakazi, a Rwandan women's rights activist noted.[37]

The failure of investigators to document gender-based crimes in war further shrouds the widespread nature of the crime. Because the testimonies are not documented, the abuse of women is overlooked. As a result, indictments for war criminals often do not include rape, further confirming to rape victims the futility of reporting the crime. Women simply conclude that reporting their cases to the Rwandan judiciary or to the International Criminal Tribunal is not worth the potential risk. Rwandan women have also expressed either no knowledge of or little confidence in the International Criminal Tribunal to address the issue of rape.

Some involved in prosecuting the genocide, both at the national and international level, have suggested that it is nearly impossible to investigate rape because Rwandan women will not talk about their ordeals. This is patently false. Rwandan women will talk, but only under certain conditions. Among other things,

---

[35]Human Rights Watch/FIDH interview, Dr. Odette Nyiramilimo, Le Bon Samaritain Clinic, Kigali, March 18, 1996.

[36]Human Rights Watch/FIDH interview, Rusatira commune, March 23, 1996.

[37]Human Rights Watch/FIDH interview, Bernadette Muhimakazi, Bon Pasteur, Kigali, March 25, 1996.

investigation of rape by the national and international justice systems is best carried out by female investigators using female interpreters. Numerous Rwandan women interviewed for this report admitted their discomfort in telling their story to a man, but were willing to speak to female investigators. Investigators taking testimonies must also be sensitive to the trauma of rape victims, since in Rwanda as throughout the world there is profound shame and stigma associated with rape. In Rwanda, this shame is compounded by a sense of guilt for having survived. If women agree to testify, mechanisms to protect rape victims must also be guaranteed. (See also, Victim and Witness Protection). Without taking steps to ensure that Rwandan women can safely give their testimonies, it is unlikely that the genocide perpetrators of rape will be held accountable.

INTERNATIONAL AND NATIONAL LEGAL PROTECTIONS
AGAINST GENDER-BASED VIOLENCE[38]

Sexual violence against women and girls in situations of armed conflict or systematic persecution constitutes a clear breach of international law. Under international law, perpetrators of sexual violence can be held accountable for rape as a war crime, as a crime against humanity, or as an act of genocide, if their actions meet the definitial elements of each. Yet, although rape and other forms of sexual violence have long been used as weapons of conflict, they have seldom been denounced or punished.[39] According to the United Nations Special Rapporteur on Violence Against Women, "[rape] remains the least condemned war crime; throughout history, the rape of hundreds of thousands of women and children in all regions of the world has been a bitter reality."[40]

Rape has long been mischaracterized and dismissed by military and political leaders as a private crime or the unfortunate behavior of a renegade soldier. Worse still, it has been accepted precisely because it is so commonplace. The fact that rape often functions in ways similar to other human rights abuse

---

[38]Much of the information in this section was published previously in *The Global Report on Women's Human Rights*, pp. 1-99.

[39]To mention only a few examples: During the Second World War, some 200,000 Korean women were forcibly held in sexual slavery to the Japanese army. During the armed conflict in Bangladesh in 1971, it is estimated that 200,000 civilian women and girls were victims of rape committed by Pakistani soldiers. Mass rape of women has been used since the beginning of the conflict in the Former Yugoslavia. Throughout the Somali conflict beginning in 1991, rival ethnic factions have used rape against rival ethnic factions. During 1992 alone, 882 women were reportedly gang-raped by Indian security forces in Jammu and Kashmir. In Peru in 1982, rape of women by security forces was a common practice in the ongoing armed conflict between the Communist Party of Peru, the Shining Path, and government counterinsurgency forces. In Myanmar, in 1992, government troops raped women in a Rohingya Muslim village after the men had been inducted into forced labor. Under the former Haitian military regime of Lt. Gen. Raoul Cédras, rape was used as a tool of political repression against female activists or female relatives of opposition members. See, *The Global Report on Women's Human Rights*, p.1-99 and Preliminary report submitted by the Special Rapporteur on Violence against Women, its Causes and Consequences (New York: United Nations Publications, 1994), E/CN.4/1995/42, pp.63-69.

[40]Preliminary report submitted by the Special Rapporteur on Violence against Women, its Causes and Consequences, Commission on Human Rights, (New York: United Nations Publications, 1994), E/CN.4/1995/42, p.64.

makes all the more striking the fact that, until recently, it has not been exposed and condemned like any other violation. The differential treatment of gender-based violence makes clear that the problem, for the most part, lies not in the absence of adequate legal prohibitions, but in the international community's willingness to tolerate sexual abuse against women.

Further, in conception and enforcement, the crime of rape is regarded in international humanitarian law not as a violent attack against women, but as a challenge to honor.[41] The word honor implies dignity and esteem, but concerning women, it also alludes to chastity, sexual virtue and good name. The reference to rape and other forms of sexual violence as an attack on women's honor is problematic in that it fails to recognize explicitly rape and other forms of sexual violence as an attack on women's physical integrity. The categorization of rape as a crime against honor as opposed to physical integrity diminishes the serious nature of the crime and further contributes to the widespread misperception that rape (i.e. an attack on honor) is an "incidental" or "lesser" crime in comparison to crimes such as torture or enslavement.[42]

As a consequence, women, whether combatants or civilians, have been targeted with sexual violence such as rape, sexual mutilation and sexual slavery, while for the most part their attackers go unpunished. Recent United Nations world conferences have underscored the seriousness and prevalence of gender-based violence in conflict and the obligation of states and the international community to take steps to prevent and punish such abuse. Both the Vienna Declaration and Programme of Action, adopted by the World Conference on Human Rights in June 1993, and the Beijing Declaration and Platform for Action adopted at the Fourth

---

[41]For example, Article 27 of the Fourth Geneva Convention prohibits "any attack of [women's] honor, in particular against rape, enforced prostitution, or any form of indecent assault." The Geneva Convention Relative to the Protection of Civilian Persons in Time of War, Aug. 12, 1949, 6 U.S.T. 3516, 75 U.N.T.S. 287, Article 27. Protocol II to the Geneva Conventions forbids rape explicitly, but characterizes it as an outrage on personal dignity rather than as a physical assault. Protocol Additional to the Geneva Conventions of 12 August 1949, and Relating to the Protection of Victims of Non-International Armed Conflicts, opened for signature December 12, 1977, Article 2(e), 1125 UNTS 3, 16 ILM 1442 (1977) [Protocol II].

[42]Catherine N. Niarchos, "Women, War, and Rape: Challenges Facing the International Criminal Tribunal for the Former Yugoslavia," *Human Rights Quarterly* (Baltimore, MD), vol. 17, 1995, pp. 672, 674.

United Nations Conference on Women in September 1995 underscore that violations against women in conflict contravene international law.[43]

Reports of the widespread of use of rape as a tactic of war in the former Yugoslavia have been instrumental in focusing attention recently on the function of rape in conflict.[44] The situation provoked international condemnation and prompted investigations into reports of rape by all parties to that conflict. The stated commitment of the judges and chief prosecutor for the International Criminal Tribunal for the Former Yugoslavia to prosecute rape, marks a critical decision not to ignore rape as a war crime.

In late 1994, the United Nations expanded the mandate of this Tribunal to investigate and prosecute violations of the laws of war that occurred during the 1994 genocide in Rwanda. The International Criminal Tribunal for Rwanda is tasked with prosecuting persons responsible for genocide, crimes against humanity, and violations of the Geneva Conventions and their Additional Protocols that occurred in 1994.[45] The Rwandan Tribunal is empowered explicitly to prosecute rape as a crime against humanity and a violation of the Geneva Conventions.

---

[43]The Vienna Declaration states that "[a]ll violations of this kind, including in particular murder, systematic rape, sexual slavery, and forced pregnancy, require a particularly effective response." (Part II, para.38). The Beijing Platform for Action notes that: "While entire communities suffer the consequences of armed conflict and terrorism, women and girls are particularly affected because of their status in society and their sex . . . . Massive violations of human rights, especially in the form of genocide, "ethnic cleansing" as a strategy of war and its consequences, rape, including systematic rape of women in war situations, creating mass exodus of refugees and displaced persons are abhorrent practices that are strongly condemned and must be immediately stopped, while perpetrators of such crimes must be punished." (Section E, paras. 131 and 136). These declarations, while not binding treaties which states ratify, set out a common international standard that states should follow.

[44]Rape was previously prosecuted at the International Military Tribunal for the Far East (the Tokyo Tribunal) which found a number of Japanese commanders guilty of violations of the laws of war. See R.J. Pritchard and S. Magbanua Zaide, eds., *Tokyo War Crimes Trial, vol. 1 (Indictment)* (1981).

[45]Article 1 of the Statute of the International Tribunal for Rwanda provides: "The International Tribunal for Rwanda shall have the power to prosecute persons responsible for serious violation of international humanitarian law committed in the territory of Rwanda and Rwandan citizens responsible for such violations committed in the territory of neighboring States, between 1 January 1994 and 31 December 1994. . . ." United Nations Security Council Resolution 955 (1994) Establishing the International Tribunal for Rwanda, Annex.

Indictments have begun to be brought by the International Criminal Tribunal for Rwanda and the Tribunal is expected to begin hearing cases in September 1996 in Arusha, Tanzania where the Tribunal is seated.

Sexual Violence as a War Crime

International humanitarian law explicitly and implicitly condemns rape and other forms of sexual violence as war crimes. The Geneva Conventions of August 12, 1949 and the Protocols Additional to the Geneva Conventions prohibit rape in both international[46] and internal conflicts. In internal conflicts, such as that which occurred in Rwanda, common article 3 of the Geneva Conventions prohibits "violence to life and person, in particular murder of all kinds, mutilation, cruel treatment and torture" as well as "outrages upon personal dignity, in particular humiliating and degrading treatment." Protocol II Additional to the Geneva Conventions, which also governs certain internal armed conflicts and which applies to the conflict in Rwanda,[47] expressly forbids "violence to the life, health and physical or mental well-being of persons, in particular murder as well as cruel treatment such as torture, mutilation" and "outrages upon personal dignity, in particular humiliating and degrading treatment, rape, enforced prostitution and any form of indecent assault," as well as "slavery and the slave trade in all their

---

[46]The Fourth Geneva Convention of 1949 states that "Women shall be especially protected against any attack on their honour, in particular against rape, enforced prostitution, or any form of indecent assault." Further, article 147 of the same convention specifies that "torture or inhuman treatment" and "willfully causing great suffering or serious injury to body or health" are war crimes, or grave breaches, of the conventions. The Geneva Convention Relative to the Protection of Civilian Persons in Time of War, August 12, 1949 [Fourth Geneva Convention], arts.27, 147, 75 U.N.T.S. 287. The International Committee of the Red Cross (ICRC) considers rape to be among the crimes identified by article 147 of the Fourth Geneva Convention as grave breaches. Theodor Meron, "Rape as a Crime Under International Humanitarian Law," *American Journal of International Law* (Washington, D.C.), vol. 87, July 1993, p. 426, citing International Committee of the Red Cross, Aide Mémoire, December 3, 1992.

[47]The Independent Commission of Experts on Rwanda concluded that both common Article 3 and Additional Protocol II apply to the Rwanda conflict. Theodor Meron, "International Criminalization of Internal Atrocities," *American Journal of International Law* (Washington, D.C.), vol. 89, no. 3, July 1995, p. 561.

forms."[48] The ICRC explains that this provision "reaffirms and supplements Common Article 3 . . . [because] it became clear that it was necessary to strengthen . . . the protection of women . . . who may also be the victims of rape, enforced prostitution or indecent assault."[49] Drawn from these provisions, the Statute of the Tribunal for Rwanda empowers the Tribunal to prosecute those responsible for, among other serious crimes, "outrages upon personal dignity, in particular humiliating and degrading treatment, rape, enforced prostitution and any form of indecent assault."

The Prosecutor for the International Criminal Tribunals for the Former Yugoslavia and Rwanda, Justice Richard Goldstone, has recognized that rape can also constitute a form of torture under the Convention against Torture and Other Cruel, Inhumane or Degrading Treatment or Punishment[50] and has stated that the

---

[48]Protocol Additional to the Geneva Conventions of 12 August 1949, and Relating to the Protection of Victims of Non-International Armed Conflicts, opened for signature December 12, 1977, Article 4(2) (a),(e) and (f), 1125 UNTS 3, 16 ILM 1442 (1977) [Protocol II].

Similar provisions which govern protection in international conflicts are contained in Protocol Additional to the Geneva Conventions of 12 August 1949, and Relating to the Protection of Victims of International Armed Conflicts, opened for signature Dec.12,1977, 1125 UNTS 3, (1977) [Protocol I]. Article 76(1) of Protocol I states that women "shall be protected in particular against rape, forced prostitution, or any form of indecent assault." Article 86(2) of Protocol I makes commanders who had information about grave breaches punishable themselves "if they did not take all feasible measures within their power to prevent or suppress" a grave breach. Article 75 expressly forbids mutilation. Also, Article 11(1) and (2) state that "physical mutilations" shall not be carried out on "persons who are in the power of the adverse Party and who are interned, detained or otherwise deprived of liberty" as a result of an international armed conflict.

[49]Yves Sandoz, Christophe Swinarski, Bruno Zimmerman, eds., *ICRC Commentary on the Additional Protocols of 8 June 1977 to the Geneva Conventions of 12 August 1949* (Geneva: Martinus Nijhoff Publishers, 1987), p. 1375, para. 4539.

[50]Convention against Torture and Other Cruel, Inhumane or Degrading Treatment or Punishment, December 10, 1984, 23 I.L.M.1027 (1984), article 1, defines torture as "any act by which severe pain or suffering, whether physical or mental, is intentionally inflicted on a person for such purposes as obtaining from him or a third person information or a confession, punishing him for an act he or a third person has committed or is suspected of having committed, or intimidating or coercing him or a third person, or for any reason based on discrimination of any kind, when such pain and suffering is inflicted by or at the instigation of or with the consent or acquiescence of a public official or other person acting

International Criminal Tribunals will prosecute rape as a form of torture where appropriate. Justice Goldstone has stated:

> Sexual assaults, committed particularly against women, can constitute torture under the Statue of the Tribunal, and will be prosecuted as transgressions of international humanitarian law by my office.

> Our legal position is also consistent with the evolving norm of torture. The Special Rapporteur on Torture in the 1986 Report identified rape and sexual assaults as common forms of torture. The Inter-American Commission of Human Rights' Report on Haiti stated that the infliction of rapes on the female civilian population, was torture. *In the Matter of Krone*, the US Immigrations Appeal Board found that a Haitian woman who was gang raped in retaliation for her political belief had been "persecuted." The sexual assaults committed during the conflict in the Former Yugoslavia and Rwanda correspondingly provide the basis for justiciable charges of torture.

> I have, therefore, requested a review of all previous indictments and, where an evidentiary base exists to charge torture, we will seek leave to amend.[51]

Sexual Violence as a Crime Against Humanity

Rape—like murder, extermination, enslavement, deportation, imprisonment, torture, persecution on political, racial and religious grounds and other inhuman acts—is a crime against humanity. Crimes against humanity arise when such serious crimes as these are committed on a mass scale against a civilian

---

in an official capacity."

[51]Letter from Justice Richard Goldstone, Prosecutor, U.N. International Criminal Tribunals for the Former Yugoslavia and Rwanda to Professor Rhonda Copelon, Professor of Law and Director, International Women's Human Rights Law Clinic, City University of New York, The Hague, September 8, 1995.

population.[52] After the Second World War, the Control Council for Germany enacted Control Council Law number 10 as a basis of establishing a uniform legal basis for the prosecution of war criminals in Germany. In the second set of Nuremberg war criminal trials, conducted under the authority of Control Council Law number 10, and in Article 6(c) of the Nuremberg Charter, rape was specifically enumerated as a crime against humanity, although rape was not prosecuted at any of these trials.[53]

The Statute of the Tribunal for Rwanda defines crimes against humanity as those crimes, including rape, that are "committed as part of a widespread or

---

[52]Under the Nuremberg Charter, crimes against humanity were punishable only if they had a nexus to war. Theodor Meron, "War Crimes in Yugoslavia and the Development of International Law," *American Journal of International Law* (Washington, D.C.), vol. 88, no.1, January 1994, pp. 84-87. Since then, no treaty has defined crimes against humanity, and the question remains as to whether crimes against humanity arise only when linked to war. The Statute of the International Criminal Tribunal for the Former Yugoslavia gives the Tribunal competence over crimes against humanity only when committed in internal or international armed conflicts. But the U.N. Secretary-General's commentary on the statute "suggests that crimes against humanity can be committed even outside international or internal armed conflicts." Theodor Meron, "International Criminalization of Internal Atrocities," *American Journal of International Law* (Washington, D.C.), vol. 89, no. 3, July 1995, p. 557. In defining the elements of crimes against humanity, Article 3 of the Rwanda Statute makes no reference to the international or internal nature of the conflict. Rather it describes as crimes against humanity crimes committed "as part of a widespread or systematic attack." According to Meron, the Rwanda Statute thus "strengthens the precedent set by the commentary to the Yugoslavia Statute and enhances the possibility of arguing in the future that crimes against humanity (in addition to genocide) can be committed even in peacetime." Meron, "International Criminalization," p. 557.

[53]Article 6(c) states that crimes against humanity are "Atrocities and offenses, including but not limited to murder, extermination, enslavement deportation, imprisonment, torture, rape or other inhuman acts committed against any civilian population or persecutions on political, racial or religious grounds in execution of or in connection with any crime within the jurisdiction of the Tribunal whether or not in violation of the domestic law of the country where perpetrated." The Nuremberg Charter, as amended by the Berlin Protocol, 59 Stat. 1546, 1547 (1945), E.A.S. No. 472, 82 U.N.T.S. 284. See generally Diane Orentlicher, "Settling Accounts: The Duty to Prosecute Human Rights Violations of a Prior Regime," *The Yale Law Journal* (New Haven, CT), vol. 100, no. 8, June 1991, p. 2537.

systematic attack against any civilian population on national, political, ethnic, racial or religious grounds."

Sexual Violence as an Act of Genocide

Rape and other acts of sexual violence can also be genocidal acts. Genocide is distinguished from other international crimes, not by the scope of the acts, but rather by the intent of the perpetrators in committing the acts to destroy a national, ethnic, racial or religious group.

The crime of genocide has been codified in the Convention on the Prevention and Punishment of the Crime of Genocide (hereinafter, the "Genocide Convention"). Article 2 provides:

> Genocide means any of the following acts committed with the intent to destroy, in whole or in part, a national, ethnic, racial or religious group, as such:
>
> (a)   Killing members of the group;
> (b)   Causing serious bodily or mental harm to members of the group;
> (c)   Deliberately inflicting on the group conditions of life calculated to bring about its physical destruction in whole or in part;
> (d)   Imposing measures intended to prevent births within the group;
> (e)   Forcibly transferring children of the group to another group.[54]

Establishing genocide requires showing that the specific intent of these actions is the destruction, in whole or in part, of a national, ethnic, racial or religious group. Merely because an act, including one of sexual violence, occurs at the same time as or in the context of genocide does not mean that it is a genocidal act. Rather, intent must be proven with respect to that category of acts, which can be done by reference to all surrounding circumstances, including explicit affirmation or a pattern of actions that clearly indicate the intent to destroy a pertinent group, in whole or in part.

---

[54]Convention on the Prevention and Punishment of the Crime of Genocide, Dec. 9, 1948, 78 U.N.T.S. 277.

Acts of rape and other forms of sexual violence can fall into the categories of proscribed acts under the Genocide Convention. Where it can be shown that perpetrators committed such acts causing serious bodily or mental harm with the intent to destroy, in whole or in part, a group identified by the terms of the convention, crimes such as rape, sexual mutilation and sexual slavery may be prosecuted under subsection (b) of Article 2. As the testimonies in this report demonstrate, extremely serious bodily and mental harm was inflicted through targeted sexual violence against women.

Moreover, under certain circumstances, sexual violence may be prosecuted under subsection (c) or (d) of Article 2. Sexual violence can inflict on a group conditions of life calculated to cause the group's physical destruction and can prevent births within the group. For example, women subjected to sexual violence may be left physically unable to reproduce, or, they may be denied this role by their community given the nature of the attacks they have suffered.

The genocidal intent behind sexual violence in the Rwandan genocide emerges from both the overall pattern of sexual violence and the individual cases of abuse, documented in different parts of the country during different phases of the genocide. The pattern of sexual violence in Rwanda shows that acts of rape and sexual mutilation were not acessory to the killings, nor, for the most part, opportunistic assaults. Rather, according to the actions and statements of the perpetrators, as recalled by survivors, these acts were carried out with the aim of eradicating the Tutsi. Taken as a whole, the evidence indicates that many rapists expected, consequent to their attacks, that the psychological and physical assault on each Tutsi woman would advance the cause of the destruction of the Tutsi people.

In individual cases documented by Human Rights Watch/FIDH, survivors testified that their attackers enunciated their intent to destroy them and their people and characterized sexual violence as a means to achieve that destruction. One rape survivor told us, "While they were raping me, they were saying that they wanted to kill all Tutsi so that in the future all that would left would be drawings to show that there were once a people called the Tutsi." Others recounted how their attackers said that rather than kill the women on the spot, they would leave them to die from their grief.

Genocidal intent may also be evident in the nature of the sexual violence in question. Sexual violence, like other forms of torture, can precede or be a medium of extrajudicial execution. And, in Rwanda, acts of sexual mutilation and other life-threatening violence were inflicted in pursuit of the victims' eventual death. Women were gang raped, raped repeatedly with objects, and subjected to outrageous brutality, some of which involved mutilating women's sexual organs.

Some of these attacks left women so physically injured that they may never be able to bear children. Many victims of sexual assault died in the course of or consequent to an attack. Sexual violence in such cases was a direct part of the killing. In other cases documented by Human Rights Watch/FIDH, women survived sexual violence because their assailants left them for dead, believing that they were mortally injured.

Rape as a Crime under Rwandan Law

Rwandan law provides for the prosecution of rape under its criminal law. Rwanda also is obligated to prosecute rape under the international conventions that it has ratified, the Geneva Conventions and their optional protocols and, for reasons outlined above, the Genocide Convention. Rape is a crime under Article 360 of the 1977 Rwandan Penal Code, and is punishable by five to ten years imprisonment.

In a long-awaited development, on August 9, 1996, the Transitional National Assembly passed new legislation for the prosecution of genocide cases and crimes against humanity committed between October 30, 1990 and December 31, 1994.[55] At this writing, the Constitutional Court has not yet ruled on this law, but is expected to do so shortly.

The legislation authorizes prosecutions against those accused of having committed acts which constitute: the crime of genocide or a crime against humanity; or offenses set out in the Penal Code which were committed in connection with the genocide and crimes against humanity. The law classifies the prosecutions into four categories, and establishes a mechanism whereby those accused under categories 2, 3 and 4 can confess their guilt and receive a reduced sentence.[56] A three-tiered system applies to each category and determines the amount of the penalty reduction, based on whether the defendant confessed before indictment, after indictment, or if a confession was not entered (which also applies if the confession was rejected).

---

[55]"Loi Organique sur l'Organisation des Poursuites des Infractions Constitutives du Crime du Genocide our de Crimes Contre l'Humanité Commises a partir du 1er Octobre 1990," adopted by the Assemblée Nationale de Transition on August 9, 1996.

[56]Human Rights Watch/FIDH do not oppose plea agreements for a reduced sentenced *per se*. However, we oppose plea agreements in cases where: 1) they result in an unacceptably low sentence, or 2) the reduced sentence undermines the full and accurate exposure of the abuses for which the defendant admits guilt.

Category 1, which carries a mandatory death penalty,[57] includes the following: a) the planners and organizers of the genocide; b) those who were in a position of authority (in political parties, the army, religious orders or militias) on the national, prefectoral, communal, or sectoral level; c) those who were killers of great renown because of the zeal or cruelty with which they carried out the killing; d) those who committed acts of sexual torture.[58] Category 2 covers perpetrators or accomplices of intentional homicide or serious assaults that resulted in death, and carries a sentence of life imprisonment; Category 3 covers persons accused of other serious assaults;[59] and Category 4 covers offenses against property.

Due to the serious lack of human and material resources available to try the 80,000 genocide cases currently pending, the new legislation provides for confession-based plea agreements. The confession program would allow any persons, except those in Category 1, to fully confess to their crime and offer to plead guilty. If the confession and guilty plea are accepted, an individual may receive a reduced sentence. If an individual confesses before being indicted under Category 2, he would receive a 7 to 11 year sentence; if he confesses after being indicted, he would receive 12 to 15 years. If he confesses before being indicted

---

[57]Human Rights Watch and FIDH oppose the infliction of capital punishment in all circumstances as a violation of the inalienable right to life, and because of its inherent cruelty. In addition, we are concerned that it is most often carried out in a discriminatory manner. Furthermore, the inherent fallibility of all criminal justice systems assures that even when full due process of law is respected innocent persons are sometimes executed. Because an execution is irreversible, such miscarriages of justice can never be corrected. Human Rights Watch and FIDH therefore object to the retention or reintroduction of the death penalty in all countries, and oppose executions under law whenever and wherever carried out, irrespective of the crime and the legal process leading to the imposition of the penalty.

[58]According to Article 9, the prosecutor's office is required to present a list to the Supreme Court, to be published three months after the publication of the genocide law and updated periodically thereafter, of all those to be prosecuted under Category 1. Once the list is published, anyone who confesses to a Category 1 crime whose confession is accepted and whose name does not appear on the updated prosecutor's list will not be prosecuted under Category 1, but instead under Category 2 (if the victim died) or Category 3. However, if it is later discovered that the person committed crimes not included in his confession, he can be prosecuted under the category appropriate to that crime.

[59]In an earlier draft of the legislation, Category 3 explicitly included rape. However, the version passed by the National Assembly omitted any mention of rape, while adding sexual torture as a Category 1 crime.

under Category 3, he would receive one-third of the sentence the court would otherwise impose; if he confesses after, he would receive half of that sentence.

At this writing, it is unclear under which category those accused of rape will be prosecuted. Clearly, many rape cases would fall under Category 1 as sexual torture. However, it is unclear whether sexual torture will be interpreted to include all acts of rape or only those with certain characteristics. In any event, given the lack of investigations thus far focusing on rape and sexual violence during the genocide, it is unlikely that rape prosecutions will be launched in the near future.

GENDER-BASED VIOLENCE AGAINST RWANDAN WOMEN

During the 1994 genocide, Rwandan women were subjected to brutal forms of sexual violence.[60] Rape was widespread.[61] Women were individually raped, gang-raped, raped with objects such as sharpened sticks or gun barrels, held in sexual slavery (collectively or individually) or sexually mutilated. In almost every case, these crimes were inflicted upon women after they had witnessed the torture and killings of their relatives, and the destruction and looting of their homes. Some women were forced to kill their own children before or after being raped. Women were raped or gang-raped repeatedly as they fled from place to place. Others were held prisoner in houses specifically for the purpose of rape for periods ranging from a few days to the duration of the genocide. Pregnant women or women who had just given birth were not spared, and these rapes often caused hemorrhaging and other medical complications which resulted in their deaths. At checkpoints and mass graves, women were pulled aside to be raped, often before being killed. Many women came close to death several times during the three month period and in some cases begged to be killed so that the suffering would end. Instead, they were often spared so they could be raped and humiliated by the genocide perpetrators. Survivors report that during the genocide, militia even raped the corpses of women they had just killed or women who had been left for

---

[60]See also, Bonnet, "Le viol des femmes survivantes du génocide du Rwanda,"; African Rights, *Rwanda: Death, Despair and Defiance*, pp. 748-797; Annie Arnou and Stev Van Thielen (directors), *Devil's Children* (video documentary), (Belgium: BRTN-NV de Wereld television station, April 1995); Coordination of Women's Advocacy, "Mission on Gender-Based War Crimes Against Women and Girls During the Genocide in Rwanda: Summary of Findings and Recommendations," Geneva, July 1995; and Ministry of Family and the Promotion of Women, "Enquête effectuée auprès des victimes".

[61]In the context of the genocide, the Kinyarwanda word *kubohoza* was used for rape. Kubohoza literally means "to help liberate." The term is used ironically. With the advent of multiparty politics in Rwanda, force was increasingly used in order to coerce people to change political parties. The term kubohoza was first used to describe this phenomenon. Later, it was used to describe the taking of land, then resources, and eventually, women. When people engaged in kubohoza, they sometimes covered their faces with chalk, wore banana leaves, attacked at the signal of a whistle, marched to a drum and manned barriers along the roads to catch their prey. The killers of the genocide did the same thing. The use of the term kubohoza for rape was a continuation of an attitude that accepted violence as normal in the pursuit of political ends.

dead. After killing women, the militia would frequently leave their corpses naked and with legs spread apart.

In many communities, rape was perpetrated largely by militia groups now known collectively as the Interahamwe, and condoned and encouraged by the army and government authorities.[62] Rapes were also committed by soldiers of the Armed Forces of Rwanda. Some women recounted how younger militia had been urged to rape the women by older militia in the group. Many of the militia were neighbors, or even friends, of the families they tortured, raped and killed. In some cases, government soldiers surrounded an area to prevent people from escaping the Hutu militia attacks.

In addition to advancing targeted attacks, the genocide planners deliberately created and permitted a generalized environment of lawlessness which also served to further their political goals. In the surrounding violence, women were targeted, regardless of their ethnicity or political affiliation. The government and military authorities gave the militias full license to commit egregious human rights abuses, including rape, with impunity. One analysis of the genocide summarized the violence that ensued as follows:

> In Kigali, the Interahamwe and Impuzamugambi ["Those who have a common purpose"] had tended to recruit mostly among the poor. As soon as they went into action, they drew around them a cloud of even poorer people, a lumpenproletariat of street boys, rag-pickers, car-washers and homeless unemployed. For these people, the genocide was the best thing that could have happened to them. They had the blessings of a form of authority to take revenge on socially powerful people as long as these were on the wrong side of the political fence. They could steal, they could kill with minimum justification, they could rape . . . This was wonderful. The political aims pursued by the masters

---

[62]The Interahamwe (Kinyarwanda for 'those who work together') were civilian Hutu militias who actively participated in the genocide, under the direction of the army and government authorities. Although the name Interahamwe officially described the youth wing of the *Mouvement Republicain Nationale Democratique* (MRND), the former ruling party, the term came to refer to all militia participating in the genocide, regardless of their party affiliation. In addition to these militia, ordinary people were mobilized with little organization or training to pillage, destroy, torture and kill.

of this dark carnival were quite beyond their scope. They just went along, knowing it would not last.[63]

The planners of the genocide capitalized on the widely held but often inaccurate belief that Tutsi were richer than Hutu. As one Rwandan woman put it, "The Interahamwe were usually young men, often just amusing themselves. Some rapes were targeted against Tutsi and opponents of the government, especially Hutu from the South. But for many Interahamwe, it was a class issue."[64]

In attacks on Tutsi before 1994, women and children were generally spared, but during the genocide—particularly in its later stages—all Tutsi were targeted, regardless of sex or age. Especially after mid-May 1994, the leaders of the genocide called on killers not to spare women and children. The widespread incidence of rape accompanied this increase in overall violence against groups previously immune from attack. "Rape was a strategy," said Bernadette Muhimakazi, a Rwandan women's rights activist. "They chose to rape. There were no mistakes. During this genocide, everything was organized. Traditionally it is not the custom to kill women and children, but this was done everywhere too."[65] Other Rwandans characterized the choice of violence against women in the following ways: "It was the humiliation of women"; or "It was the disfigurement of women, to make them undesirable, used"; or, finally, "Women's worth was not respected."

Both Tutsi and Hutu women were raped, but there was a difference both in the numbers assaulted and in the reasons for the rapes. Most of the women raped were Tutsi and they were attacked as one more means of terrorizing and destroying the Tutsi ethnic group. Hutu women, fewer in number, were targeted ordinarily because they were close to Tutsi: either wives of Tutsi men, supporters of political groups associated with Tutsi, or protectors of Tutsi. Some women were simply caught in the general increase in violence.

---

[63]Gérard Prunier, *The Rwanda Crisis: History of a Genocide*, (New York: Columbia University Press, 1995), pp. 231-232.

[64]Human Rights Watch/FIDH interview, Kigali, March 18, 1996.

[65]Human Rights Watch/FIDH interview, Bernadette Muhimakazi, Bon Pasteur, Kigali, March 25, 1996.

Sexual Violence Against Tutsi Women

Rape by the Militia

Since the militia were working in groups, Tutsi women who were taken from their homes or found hiding were frequently subjected to gang-rape. Often, women were raped multiple times. Many survived one rape or gang-rape, only to be discovered by another group of Interahamwe who would rape them again. Frequently, women were killed immediately following the rape. The following accounts are from survivors who were raped because they were Tutsi women: [66]

Bernadette was thirty-three years old and living in Taba commune, Gitarama prefecture, when the fighting began. She recalled that she, her husband and seven children hid in nearby coffee bushes when the Interahamwe first came to their area on April 12, 1994. They hid, listening to the militia killing, destroying and looting all the houses. In the evening, they were discovered by a group of about fifty militia armed with machetes, knives and hoes. They took Bernadette and her family to the Nyabarongo River. She said:

> The next day, they killed all the men and boys. I was left with my baby and the three girls. At the riverside, I was raped by a group of six Interahamwe one after another. I knew all of them. Some were killed by the RPF and the others are now in Gitarama prison. They said that they were raping me to see if Tutsi women were like Hutu women. After they finished raping me, they threw me in the river to die along with my children. My children all drowned, but the river threw me back. I floated back to the riverside. One of the Interahamwe said, "Those Tutsi people won't die—we raped her and she survived. We threw her in the river and she still survived." They let me go and I tried to go toward Runda commune (the next commune). On the way, I was found by another group of Interahamwe who took me with them back to Taba. They also raped me. I can't remember how many. After the war, I found out that I was pregnant. But I had

---

[66]The names of all the rape survivors interviewed have been changed in order to protect their safety and privacy.

an abortion . . . no, not really an abortion. The baby just came out dead.[67]

Perpetue was twenty years old and living in Runda commune, Gitarama prefecture, with her husband and child and her sister when the violence began. She hid in neighboring Taba commune until the militia groups from Taba and Runda communes began working together to find out who they had missed in the area. Perpetue was soon discovered by the militia and survived a horrific three months in which she was raped multiple times and her vagina was mutilated. She said:

> On April 9, 1994, they found me. I was taken to the Nyabarongo River by a group of Interahamwe. When I got there, one Interahamwe said to me that he knew the best method to check that Tutsi women were like Hutu women. For two days, myself and eight other young women were held and raped by Interahamwe, one after another. Perhaps as many as twenty of them. I knew three of them. Some Interahamwe watched over us while others went to eat and sleep. All the young women killed at that river were raped before being thrown in. I didn't know any of the other women. On the third day, one Interahamwe saw that I was not able to walk anymore. He told me that I had already died and could go. I tried to leave, but I could barely walk. There was blood everywhere and my stomach hurt. I walked towards Kamonyi and found refuge in an old church there. When I was going there, I saw that the Interahamwe had been burning people to death. I saw at least ten burnt bodies.
>
> I was in the church building when the Interahamwe came there on May 15 and told us that it was our turn to be burnt. They took a lot of people outside to kill them. One Interahamwe chose me, but told me that he would protect me so that I would not be burnt to death. He took me to another building near the church and raped me there. Before he raped me, he said that he wanted to check if Tutsi women were like other women before he took me back to the church to be burnt. There were other

---

[67]Human Rights Watch/FIDH interview, Taba commune, Gitarama prefecture, April 9, 1996.

women being raped there at the same time, maybe ten women and seven young girls. The next day, two Interahamwe watched over us while the others went to kill. The two were complaining they were feeling tired from all the killing. Then, one of them sharpened the end of the stick of a hoe. They held open my legs and pushed the stick into me. I was screaming. They did it three times until I was bleeding everywhere. Then they told me to leave. I tried to stand up, but I kept falling down. Finally I crawled outside. I was naked crawling on the ground covered in blood. I tried to ask someone on the road for help, but they thought I was a madwoman and just ignored me. I finally found a house where they gave me some medicine to apply to the area between my legs. They also gave me some clothes, but because I was bleeding so much the skirt became soaked with blood.[68]

Perpetue stayed hiding in the bush for about one week until she found two men with a bicycle who were willing to take her to Gisenyi in the north-west part of the country. She thought that if she left the area where she was originally from, she would not be recognized as a Tutsi. Unfortunately, when she arrived in Gisenyi at the end of May, she was recognized by an Interahamwe from her home area. He immediately notified the other militia that she was Tutsi and she was taken to a mass grave. Perpetue continued to recount her experience:

I was told to give my clothes to them. The mass grave was for women and girls only and it was being organized by a woman they called Donatha. She had a long knife and cut me immediately behind the knee. One Interahamwe saw me and took me aside along with four other women. He explained to us that all the Gitarama people were going to be killed, but that he would protect us and that we could live with him. He took me to the lake. There, he raped me. I cried out because I was still wounded from before and he was opening all the wounds again. He beat me for crying and gagged my mouth. He told me that I was forbidden to cry because Tutsi had no rights at that moment. He also said that any Tutsi woman from Gitarama would be killed in an even worse way than what he was doing to

_____

[68]Human Rights Watch/FIDH interview, Taba commune, Gitarama prefecture, April 9, 1996.

me. After the rape, I was left alone and naked. I decided to try and escape. I couldn't walk properly and so I was on all fours. When people passed me, I sat down and stopped walking so they wouldn't know that I had been raped because I was ashamed. I crawled like that for two days in the bush. When I urinated, it came out like blood. Black, coagulated blood kept coming out of my vagina.

When I got to the road (later I found that I had been walking south along the Rwanda-Zaire border towards Kibuye) I found a camp—Rubengera camp—which was being run by the French. But I recognized someone there who had killed my family so I left. I survived for three days in the bush before the RPF came. When I saw the RPF fighters, I thought it was the Interahamwe. I told them to kill me because I didn't care anymore. They took me to Kibuye where I was examined by a French doctor and was given medicine, food and clothes. When they gave me underwear, it was so painful that I could not even put it on. I was given medical care from June 1994 to December 1994. I had to sit in medicated baths every day. They offered to send me to France for medical treatment, but I wanted to go back to my home. Since the war has ended, I have not had my monthly period. My stomach sometimes swells up and is painful. I think about what has happened to me all the time and at night I cannot sleep. I even see some of the Interahamwe who did these things to me and others around here. When I see them, I think about committing suicide.

Elizabeth was twenty-nine years old and living in Kigali with her husband when the killing began. The militia came to their house while they were eating dinner with a group of people. She said:

About ten of them came. They picked two of the women in the group: a twenty-five year old and a thirty year old and then gang-raped them. When they finished, they cut them with knives all over while the other Interahamwe watched. Then they took the food from the table and stuffed it into their vaginas. The women died. They were left dead with their legs spread apart. My husband tried to put their legs together before we were told to get out of the house, and to leave the children behind. They killed two of our children. My husband begged them not to kill us, saying that he did not have any money on him, but that he had shoes and second-hand clothes that he sells at the market. He gave them all the clothes. Then, one Interahamwe said "you Tutsi women are very sweet, so we have to kill the man and take you." [69]

Elizabeth's husband was killed and she was taken by the head of the militia to his house where she was raped. Ultimately, she managed to escape. She currently has no house and takes care of eight children—two of her own and six orphaned relatives. When asked about prosecuting those who raped her, Elizabeth said, "How can they be prosecuted? They are not even here."

Marie-Claire recounted how she was attacked by the military and the militia: "We were attacked by military together with Interahamwe. The Interahamwe were sent by the military. The Interahamwe were wild. To survive, you had to let yourself be raped. They told me to give them my money or my children." All but one of her children were killed by the militia. Marie-Claire was raped by a militia man whom she knew, a neighbor. "He is in Zaire now," she said. She continued:

He said many things during the rape and he hit and kicked me. He said "we have all the rights over you and we can do whatever we want." They had all the power—our men, our husbands, were all exterminated. We have no mother, no father, no brothers.[70]

Clementine and her husband and three children were separated as they fled from the militia in Kayenzi commune, Gitarama prefecture. After hiding for two days, thirty-eight-year-old Clementine was found by the militia one night as she hid in the bushes. They beat her badly before five of them raped both her and another woman hiding with her. "Two of the older militia refused to rape me," she said, "but they urged the younger ones to rape me and the other woman with me.

---

[69]Human Rights Watch/FIDH interview, Kigali, April 4, 1996.

[70]Human Rights Watch/FIDH interview, Taba commune, Gitarama prefecture, March 26, 1996.

They were saying "we want to see how the *Tutsikazi*[71] look inside." "You can't shout—you must accept everything that we do to you now." After finishing the rapes, the older militia told the younger ones not to bother to kill Clementine because "you've already killed her." However, they killed the other rape victim before leaving the area. Clementine wandered around dazed looking for someone to help her. She knocked on the door of one house and when the owner opened the door, he said "you Tutsikazi are still alive. Why didn't they kill you?" Clementine later found refuge in the house of a woman who hid her until the RPF came in July 1994. Clementine continues to have back and internal problems. She also has frequent nightmares and constantly forgets things. However, she had not had any medical treatment because she has no money.[72]

   Josepha was thirty-eight years old and living in Shyanda commune, Butare prefecture, in 1994. Her family was attacked by the militia in April 1994 and many were killed. She hid in the sorghum fields, but was caught by the militia. They hit her over the head, and took her by the arms and legs and threw her in the air. She fell on the ground on top of some broken bottles. Then two of the militia raped her. One of them has not been arrested and continues to live in Butare. Josepha said, "rape is a crime worse than death." She has not returned to her land or her house, but stays in a camp for widows with her one surviving daughter.[73]

   Goretti, a twenty-six-year-old woman from Rusatira commune, Butare prefecture, was raped several times during the course of the genocide. When the violence began, the militia, who were all neighbors and even friends, told the women to go back to their land because they "did not have ethnicity"[74] and that they were only killing the men. Nonetheless, after all her family was killed, she decided to hide in the bushes. She was soon discovered and held by a militiaman who raped her repeatedly over a period of two weeks. After the genocide, this man was arrested. Goretti explained how the militia behaved:

---

[71] *Tutsikazi* is the Kinyarwanda word for Tutsi woman.

[72] Human Rights Watch/FIDH interview, Kayenzi commune, Gitarama prefecture, March 26, 1996.

[73] Human Rights Watch/FIDH interview, Shyanda commune, Butare prefecture, April 2, 1996.

[74] As noted above, the general killing of women and children began in many areas only after the middle of May, 1994.

The Interahamwe shared women. Each one took a woman or a girl. The Interahamwe chased young girls and women—most were taken by two militia. I was taken by one who kept me for two weeks in mid-May. He told me that he would kill me after two weeks. Then he got tired of me and kicked me out.

Goretti was raped a second time after she managed to escape to near-by Songa. She was discovered by dogs that were sent to sniff out people hiding in the bush. She was caught and raped by two of the militia whom she did not recognize. She said:

I was taken by force—they were like wild animals. You knew it was your last days, but I fought back anyway. They said that they had to take Tutsi women because before the war they were not able to take them. They said that Tutsi women stayed to themselves before.

Goretti concluded by saying that "most women were raped, if they are still alive. They [the Interahamwe] did whatever they wanted." She continued softly, "You can't ever forget. Now there's no one. Until I die, I'll always be sad."[75]

Rape by the Military

Military as well as civilian authorities encouraged or condoned rape, murder and other violence by militia groups and others. The military included regular soldiers, members of the national police force, and members of the elite Presidential Guard. The civilian authorities included burgomasters, communal councillors and heads of sectors. They distributed arms, led meetings where people were incited to violence, and sometimes personally led attacks. Soldiers and national police ordered potential victims to stay in their homes and established roadblocks to confine targeted people to areas where they could be more easily attacked. Often the military backed up attacks by militia and other civilians, shooting those who tried to escape. In some cases, soldiers or national policemen were responsible for committing rape and murder themselves.

Chantalle was two months pregnant, twenty-eight years old and living in Kanzenze commune, Kigali prefecture, with her Hutu husband when the violence began. Her husband immediately chased her out of the house because she was

---

[75]Human Rights Watch/FIDH interview, Rusatira commune, Butare prefecture, March 23, 1996.

Tutsi telling her "I don't want to die. If you die, it is your problem." She fled with her six-year-old boy. When the RPF came to the area, her husband left for Zaire and she later heard that he had become sick and died in Zaire. Chantalle recounted her experience:

> The Presidential Guard killed here. They did whatever they wanted. They did terrible things and then they would kill you. If you were lucky, you were thrown into a communal grave. I spent one week in a communal grave, left for dead. Then an Interahamwe noticed I was still alive and pulled me out. He said that they would kill me tomorrow. I told him to kill me now. I begged him to stab me in the stomach so I would die. But he let me go and even gave me some water. The Presidential Guard and the Interahamwe killed many people. They even raped the corpses. They were like wild animals. I was raped by a soldier from the Presidential Guard. I saw his uniform even though he was covered with banana leaves. I was hiding in the bush when he found me. It was broad daylight. He took me while others were running away—I could not even scream. He said, "you Tutsi are *inyenzis* [cockroaches] with long tails. We must kill Tutsi women, we must rip them apart." I also saw terrible things. I saw one woman ripped apart and hung. One leg was in one place, the other leg in another. [76]

Liberata was eighteen years old when the violence began in Butare prefecture. Three days after the President's plane was shot down, soldiers came to her house, assured her family that they would be safe and told them to remain in the house where she was living with her mother, sisters and brother. The soldiers returned at night with six Interahamwe who were armed with machetes and guns. Liberata managed to escape through a window while the militia killed her family with machetes. She watched them loot the house until she was discovered. The militia were about to kill her when one of the militia, who had worked as a watchman in her father's garage, told them not to kill her. He took her to the house of a friend where she stayed for three days until another militia group came looking for Tutsi. At first, they accepted money to leave the house, but after a few times, they threatened to kill the Hutu woman for protecting Liberata.

---

[76]Human Rights Watch/FIDH interview, Kanzenze commune, Kigali prefecture, March 29, 1996.

Liberata was moved to the house of another Hutu who hid her in a hole which he dug in the living room floor. For four days, she stayed in the hole, which was covered with a carpet and a table. At night, she would come out to eat and sleep. On May 8, 1994, a person who cleaned the house reported her presence to the militia. A group of approximately thirty militia stormed the house, went straight to the hiding place and dragged Liberata out. She was saved yet again because one of the militia knew her. He took her to one of his relatives in near-by Shyanda commune. Shortly after Liberata arrived in Shyanda, another group of about ten militia armed with machetes, guns and sticks found her. She tried to deny that she was Tutsi, but was dragged outside, brutally beaten on the back and neck, and gang-raped. She said:

> I begged them to stop and told them that I was not Tutsi. They said that they would return and they wanted me to find my ID card to show them. Then on June 30, the RPF came to Savé [Shyanda commune] and the Hutu fled to Zaire. The Hutu family that was protecting me wanted me to go to Zaire with them. But I refused. Before the war I was a student. Now I live with this woman, but she has no money to send me to school.[77]

Virginie was twenty-three years old when she sought refuge at the Agricultural Research Center (ISAR) at Rubona, Butare prefecture, along with hundreds of other Tutsi during the genocide. During that time, according to Virginie, machetes and other weapons were being distributed by the commune head as well as the sector head, Ngirabega, to Hutu in the area. On April 25, 1994, the militia and soldiers from the Armed Forces surrounded ISAR and attacked it.

> They started shooting, so I ran outside the compound. Outside, there were Interahamwe with machetes. I was with my husband, my brother-in-law and my three children who were five months old, four and six years old. My husband told us to separate so we could have a chance to survive. I took the baby and walked to the next commune. When I got there, I found out that my husband and children had been killed. The people in the area told me to give myself up to the militias. On April 26, 1994, a group of Interahamwe found me. They decided to take me to the

---

[77]Human Rights Watch/FIDH interview, Rusatira commune, Butare prefecture, March 23, 1996.

head of their group. Six of them with machetes began to take me there. As we were walking, I saw the body of my child dead on the side of the road. I refused to go on. I wanted to die right there near the body of my child in the rain. Other Interahamwe came. They stripped me naked and took all my money. Then they told me that they were going to take me to my house so they could loot it. At the house, they killed the baby on my back and then five of them raped me. They said, "we want to see how a Tutsi can die." Then, they told me to go away, because other people would kill me in time. I ran until I finally got to a friend's house. They protected me until the RPF came.[78]

Consilda, a thirty-eight-year-old woman, hid in the sorghum when the violence began. She explained that in her area the fighting started when interim President Theodore Sindikubwabo, who was appointed after the death of President Habyarimana, came to Cyamukuza sector, Ndora commune, Butare prefecture, with a truck full of Presidential Guard soldiers. The Tutsi who had sought refuge at the commune office were all put into a house and surrounded by the militia. They looked for the Presidential Guard to conduct the killing, but the Presidential Guard told the militia to do it. The house was doused with gasoline and the Tutsi inside burnt to death. While this was happening, Consilda remained in hiding in the sorghum field with her three children, ages six, three and one month. She decided to walk to Shyanda commune, Butare prefecture, where she was originally from, hoping it was calmer there. She had a number of encounters with the militia along the way. When she reached a roadblock at Ndora commune, which borders Shyanda commune, on May 3, 1994 she asked for something to drink. The militia at the roadblock gang-raped her. "Eight young men did bad things. I couldn't breathe," she said. She knew all eight men since most were neighbors of her family. After raping her, they told her, "we thought Tutsi women were different, but we found they are just the same." Consilda was hurt and swollen all over. She attempted to escape, but they speared her and hit her head with an ubuhiri, a small nail-studded club, until she fainted. Finally, one of the men took pity on her and

----

[78]Human Rights Watch/FIDH interview, Rusatira commune, Butare prefecture, March 23, 1996.

took her to a house. There she learned that her sister had been killed with an arrow shoved up her vagina.[79]

Anne, a thirty-eight-year-old widow from Shyanda commune, Butare prefecture, suffered at the hands of the militia and soldiers. When the fighting began, her house was burnt down by the militia and she and her four children (ages nine to twenty) fled. They hid in the bushes for a week while people were being slaughtered around them, until they were discovered by a group of soldiers and militia who were using dogs to track down people hiding in the bushes. Anne said:

> The Interahamwe were wearing banana leaves around their waist and on their head and across their chests. They stripped us of all our clothes. At that time, I do not even think I could call myself a person. I had not eaten for a week. I had not washed. They killed all my children in front of me and they slashed my right arm. The Presidential Guard was telling them to take all the property of the Tutsi and to do what they wanted. That included rape. After that, the Presidential Guard left the Interahamwe alone. Two of the Interahamwe raped me. I know who they were. One is now in Burundi. While they were raping me, they were saying that they wanted to kill all Tutsi so that in the future all that would be left would be drawings to show that there were once a people called the Tutsi. After the rape, I was torn and was bleeding for almost a month. My lower back was in pain. I was told to leave the area by the Interahamwe when they finished raping me. My home area before my marriage was Ndora commune, Butare prefecture, so I decided to try and go there. When I got there, I found my eldest sister and people helped us hide. I stayed there from May to July 1994 until the RPF saved us.[80]

Collective Sexual Slavery

Many women were subjected to rape and gang-rape while being held collectively by a militia group in order to sexually service the group. The women

---

[79]Human Rights Watch/FIDH interview, Shyanda commune, Butare prefecture, April 2, 1996.

[80]Human Rights Watch/FIDH interview, Shyanda commune, Butare prefecture, April 1, 1996.

were held for periods lasting as long as the duration of the genocide. Some of these women were taken forcibly to neighboring countries by the militia when they fled Rwanda at the end of the genocide. While some of these women have managed to escape back to Rwanda, others continue to remain effectively as prisoners. Still others have resigned themselves to the situation and have written letters to their family in Rwanda saying that they are still alive and that they are "married" to a man in the refugee camp in Zaire.

Marie was raped and held collectively with other women in sexual slavery. Almost all her family was killed by the militia on April 18, 1994 before she fled to Musambira commune, Gitarama prefecture, to hide with a family friend. Eventually, she was discovered by militia and taken to the local government commune office where she was held with other Tutsi for two days. Armed Forces soldiers guarded the commune office and shot those who tried to escape. The Tutsi men who were being held were eventually shot and the women were called out to bury their husbands. "We buried all the men on a Saturday morning—hundreds of men," said Marie. She continued:

> They took the women to the bush and told us that they were going to kill us. They started to beat us. Some women were beaten to death. Then they took those of us who were still alive and forced us to walk to Nyamabuye [the neighboring commune]. There were about 200 women from two communes. They chose the young women. They raped many of us. They were saying "we want a Tutsi wife." When we reached Musumba sector, they said that they were going to leave us inyenzis [cockroaches]. They kept asking us "How do you want to die?" They kept threatening that they were going to rape all of us and that they were going to beat us to death. They kept hitting us and then they took us towards Kabgayi. They said that they wanted to rape us when we got there. When we reached there they took our clothes and made all of us sit down in a big area. At night they came around with torches to look for the beautiful women. They shone the torches in our faces and they kept saying "you come, you come." The first time they chose six women. They were all raped by up to five militia. They kept changing the women through the night. When they chose me, I begged them, "please kill me." I was raped by three men. The third man was kinder to me. He gave me a T-shirt to wear after raping me. The Interahamwe in charge of the group told us that

even if they were going to kill us, first, they wanted to rape us because Tutsikazi are beautiful. The next day after I was raped, all the women were forced by the Interahamwe to walk on the road naked like a group of cattle. At all the roadblocks that we passed, the other Interahamwe were shouting to them "kill them, you have to kill them. They will make Tutsi babies." Those Interahamwe who were keeping us for rape would answer that they would kill us later. By this time, we all smelt because we had not washed. We had no clothes. We were covered with blood. Blood was everywhere. When I urinated, blood was coming out. Some women were dying of exhaustion. The Interahamwe made us sing militia songs while we walked. By the time the group reached Kabgayi, only approximately thirty women had survived the ordeal. We were held there by the militia for close to one month with other Tutsi until the RPF came into the area on June 2, 1994. "During that time," Marie said, "they would come and rape the women whenever they wanted. Luckily, I was not raped again and I was able to get some medical treatment."[81]

Constance was four months pregnant when the killing began. On April 27, 1994, a group of about thirty militia came to the house where she lived with her husband and child and looted everything. She described them:

They had banana leaves draped over their shoulders and on their head and waist. They carried machetes, hoes and spears. After they left, my husband planned to commit suicide. But the next day they came back and killed him. I was hiding and could see them killing my husband. They took all his clothes and money after killing him. I recognized one of the killers (who is now in jail). I decided to try and hide at a neighbor's house. It was raining. I was pregnant and I was trying to carry my other child. Before I could get to the neighbors, I was found by a group of Interahamwe. They ordered me and some other people I was with out of the bushes. They killed all the men and children right away and said that we three women would be killed the

---

[81]Human Rights Watch/FIDH interview, Taba commune, Gitarama prefecture, March 26, 1996.

following day. They made us bury the men and then took us with them to the market at Kimana then to Kibirizi. By this time, we were all naked because they stripped us. They took us to an old bar/cabaret, which used to be owned by a man named Ndayisaba, and locked us in there. It was a big room. In the small attached storeroom, the dead body of the owner was rotting. There were many other women held in there. The Interahamwe would come whenever they wanted and take us outside to rape. There were women from ages fifteen to fifty in there. The women there had all been raped. Some were bleeding. Others had been beaten to force them to submit. I was there two days. The first night, two men came and raped me.

Over time, all the women became weaker and weaker because we had not been given any food. The Interahamwe told us that they would kill us before we died of hunger, but that they wanted to make us suffer more. They would take us outside to rape and then bring us back in afterwards. We were then all taken to Rubona on foot. Some of the women were so exhausted that they collapsed on the road of hunger and exhaustion.

Constance and the other women were taken to the agricultural research center at Rubona (ISAR) where they were told to register (for food and clothing) by the militia. However, she suspected that the registration was really to check which Tutsi were seeking refuge there so the militia could verify whom they had missed killing and where they were located. Constance managed to escape and get to Rukubiro school, but she was found and taken back to her own commune by a group of militia. Her ordeal continued and she was raped again:

When we reached Mugogwe, they killed everyone. I was cut on the head with a machete and left because they thought I was dead. I was put into a mass grave that night and when I regained consciousness, I got out of the grave and ran in the bushes. I was trying to go to Shyanda commune, but I was stopped at a roadblock. I told them I was Hutu, but they told me to show them my fingers and said that my fingers were too long to be Hutu. Then, they told me to show them what I used to do to my husband. These Interahamwe called over the young men, some as young as twelve years old. Four of them raped me while six older Interahamwe watched and encouraged them. The smallest boys were not even able to do anything. Then after that, the Interahamwe told me to go because I probably had AIDS because I was so thin. I managed to get to Shyanda and found two of my brothers.[82]

Individual Sexual Slavery: Forced "Marriage"

As militia killed and pillaged, their members often singled out women to be held for their personal sexual service. They locked these women in their own homes or in the captors' homes, sometimes briefly, sometimes for the duration of the genocide. Such women were often called "women of the ceiling" because captors hid them in a space between the roof and the ceiling to prevent their being discovered and killed by others. The arrangement was sometimes referred to as "forced marriages" and the women so held as "wives," but these terms obfuscate the total lack of consent by the women and the coercive conditions under which they were held. These women were in fact captives, looted possessions of the militiamen, held in sexual slavery.[83]

Many of the women who were held in these forced "marriages," show enormous internal conflict when they describe the situation. On the one hand, they had no choice and in most cases despise the man whom they refer to as their "husband." On the other hand, they also realize that without the protection of this very man (who in many cases murdered the rest of their family), they would most probably be dead today. Many of these women suffer extreme guilt for having survived, particularly when the rest of their families are now dead. This sentiment is further reinforced by many of the Tutsi returnees from Zaire, Burundi or Uganda who accuse these women of having "collaborated" with the Hutu militias.

Ancille, a twenty-three-year-old woman, was at home with her mother and four brothers when about forty militia armed with machetes, sticks and nail-studded clubs stormed into the house. They immediately killed Ancille's mother and brothers in front of her, looted everything and then burnt the house. She knew some of the attackers. Then, she explained:

---

[82]Human Rights Watch/FIDH interview, Shyanda commune, Butare prefecture, April 2, 1996.

[83]See also, Bonnet, "Le viol des femmes survivantes du genocide du Rwanda," p. 19.

One of the Interahamwe started hitting me. He cut me on the leg and told me that I was going to be his wife. I had seen him before because he was from Shyanda commune. He took me to his house and other Interahamwe came to look at me. He would lock me in the house in the day and in the evening he would come home and I would be his wife. Three times during the time that this Interahamwe kept me, other groups of Interahamwe came and found me. They brought me out and took me to a mass grave nearby. But all three times, he saw me and saved my life. Sometimes he was kind to me and he told me once that if I died he would bury me. In Rwanda, it is important to be buried. Other times, he would become angry and shout at me for sitting and spending the day thinking about my dead family. He told me that I should cook for him. I wouldn't say that I was taken by force. I did it to save my life. He was my husband. I lived like that until July when the RPF came and arrested him. I heard that he was arrested and later killed. When he was taken, I was one month pregnant. As soon as he was arrested, his family told me to leave his house and accused me of being connected to the RPF. I am now staying with some friends. I delivered my baby in March 1995 and the baby died after one month.[84]

When asked whether she really considered this militia man to be her husband or whether she just called him that, Ancille replied: "When my family was killed and I was taken like this, I thought that I would have to live with this man forever because I had no one else to go to." Later on in the interview, she suddenly interrupted and returned abruptly to the subject:

. . . You know . . . we call these men our husbands. But they were not a true love. I hated this man. Maybe later on you could even be killed by them. Before the war I had a fiancée . . . This happened to a lot of young girls—even school girls around eighteen years old were kept like this. In my commune I know of three women. One of these women is still with her "husband." People say that he didn't kill anyone.

[84]Human Rights Watch/FIDH interview, Shyanda commune, Butare prefecture, April 2, 1996.

Young girls were not spared from being held in this manner. **Nadia** was still traumatized two years later. In a tearful interview during which she barely looked up, she described her experience of being raped, while only eleven years old. The militia attacked her house, and although she thought she recognized some of them, she was not sure because their faces were covered in a chalky paste. They carried machetes and nail-studded clubs. Nadia's parents and brothers were hacked to pieces in front of her. Then, one of the militia said, "don't kill the girl. I am going to take her and kill her myself." He told her that he was taking her as his wife. Nadia was taken to his house where she was locked in the kitchen.

> He only came to rape me, he never brought any food. He came about five times. He would say, "lie down or I'll kill you." So I was afraid. I would just go to the bed. He threatened to kill me with his machete. He would keep the machete near the bed while he raped me. I have never told anyone before what had happened to me. I am ashamed and scared that people will laugh at me.[85]

After two weeks, Nadia was able to escape. She does not know where her captor is now. Nadia is living in Rusatira commune with an older widow who has given her shelter. However, she has not returned to school because the widow who is keeping her cannot afford school fees.

Donnatilla lost her family and their cattle when the militia attacked Rusatira commune where she was spared because one of the militia wanted to rape her. He kept twenty-two-year-old Donnatilla for a few days and then chased her out, telling her that she would be killed by someone else even if he did not do it.[86]

In one case, a militia leader in the commune of Kigarama parceled out young women to members of his militia group who had performed their killing responsibilities particularly well. In a bizarre "marriage" ceremony, the militia leader officiated over four marriages of young girls between the ages of sixteen and nineteen years to members of his militia group.

Jeanne, one of the young women who was abducted and married in this manner, described what occurred:

---

[85]Human Rights Watch/FIDH interview, Rusatira commune, Butare prefecture, March 23, 1996.

[86]Human Rights Watch/FIDH interview, Rusatira commune, Butare prefecture, March 23, 1996.

> I knew I was condemned to this . . . I thought this is a death, like
> other deaths . . . I thought to be taken as a wife is a form of
> death. Rape is a crime worse than others. There's no death
> worse than that. The problem is that women and girls don't say
> what happened to them.[87]

When the fighting began in the south-eastern prefecture of Kibungo, nineteen-year-old Jeanne and her two sisters, ages seventeen and thirteen, were separated from the rest of her family. They took refuge in a nearby woods. While hiding, they overheard some militia talking and learned that their family had been killed, their house destroyed and the militia were looking for the rest of them. She knew some of them, but not all. She and her sisters then went to another wooded area, and ran into someone who used to watch their cows. He confirmed what had happened and told them that the militia were looking for them. He hid them and brought food at night, but was unable to do much more for fear that the Interahamwe would find out. After a week, the three sisters made their way to their grandparents' house. They found the house destroyed, and their grandparents' dead bodies lying on the floor. They went to the neighbors, who refused to hide them. Exhausted and hungry, the girls told the neighbors either to hand them over or to help them. The neighbors called the militia. The militia took the three sisters to the house of the head of the militia (a former neighbor). There, they were locked up with three of their cousins, all girls, ages fifteen, seventeen and eighteen. The militia told them that a local official had instructed them not to kill the young girls.

Shortly afterwards, a meeting was called for the militia from three sectors—Vumwe, Kansana and Kaberangwe. All six girls were brought before the meeting and asked how they had survived and who had helped them. They responded, by saying: "we are here because we were starving in the woods. Either kill us or let us go.' The head of the militia, Bonaventure Mutabazi, decreed that the four older girls would be given as wives to those militia who had killed a lot—as a prize. The two younger girls would continue to be confined and guarded by the militia. The following day, a marriage celebration was held. The militia conducted the ceremony themselves. The head of the militia decided which girl would be given to which militia member. Jeanne said:

> Bonaventure Mutabazi already had two wives, but he took me.
> The others were given to the militia without wives, who then

---

[87]Human Rights Watch/FIDH interview, Birenga Commune, Kibungo prefecture, March 31, 1996.

took them back to their houses. The two youngest ones were
sent to stay in a neighbor's house. After that, I began a new life.
I worked in the fields and in the house. I asked to go see the
area where I was from, but he refused. We were told that our
family's land would be split among our husbands. We spent two
weeks as "wives." I thought that I would live like that until my
death. All four of us were kept separately. We weren't allowed
to see or speak to each other.[88]

During the time that Jeanne was held captive, the militia would come to
the house and brag about what they had done. She recounted:

They would say things like "a certain girl was too proud—so we
raped her and then killed her." Others would just talk about how
they had raped. They would say "we wanted to see how Tutsi
look. We want to see the buttocks of a Tutsi." They talked
about cutting open a pregnant woman just to see the child's
position inside. They told me that they would leave me alive
because my parents were intelligent so I would make smart
babies.

In a twist of fate, Jeanne was finally rescued by her brother, an RPF
fighter, who came looking for her and her sisters. She said:

One day, I heard shooting. The Interahamwe told us that we had
to flee with them. My brother, who was an RPF soldier, had
found an Interahamwe who told him where we were. Since my
brother knew the area, he came straight to the house where I was
being held. There were many Interahamwe there because that
was also where they sold beer. I was inside the house, watching
the second wife's children, when I heard people running. The
RPF began shooting, and even the women ran away, leaving
their children behind. I decided to stay where I was, so at least
I'd be killed by a bullet. The RPF fighters called me, and I saw
my brother. He didn't even say hello—he just said "tell me
where the others are." It was a miracle. We had to move quickly

---

[88]Human Rights Watch/FIDH interview, Birenga Commune, Kibungo prefecture,
March 31, 1996.

to get the others or they would be taken away. We began at the house where my cousins were. We told them to come and to help look for the others. My two other sisters were being abducted by a group of militia who were fleeing the RPF. My brother saw them and warned the group that if they didn't let them go, things would happen to them. My sisters could not respond or the militia would kill them. They finally released them, although the "husband" of the younger one tried to stop her.

A number of women have continued to live with the militiamen who abducted, raped and held them during the genocide. Unfortunately, many rape survivors who now lack family, skills, and resources, consider such arrangements their best hope for economic and physical security. While some women have escaped and returned to Rwanda, some relatives report that they have received letters from their sister, daughter or niece in Zaire saying that they are alive and are "married" to a man in the camp.

Venautie was twenty-three years old when her family was killed on April 28, 1994 and she was raped by two militia members—both of whom were neighbors. She was still living with the second man when we interviewed her. During the genocide, a militia group found her hiding and accused her of having an RPF fiancé. She was handed a hoe and told to dig her own grave before they would kill her. One of the militia decided that he wanted her. The other militia told him that he had to kill her brothers in her presence before taking her. After killing her three brothers, he took her home. When Venautie reached his home, she pleaded: "I beg you to help me. Hide me. Please don't do bad things to me, don't rape me. If I survive, I'll be very grateful." He refused, saying "If there were peace, you would never accept me" before raping her. She struggled and he hit her on the head, causing an injury from which she still suffers. The following day, May 16, the head of the militia group came to the house and exercised his rank to take Venautie as his "wife." Venautie is still living with him and they have a nine-month old child. She said:

> I still live with him, and I think of him as my husband because he gives me food and lodging. Every day [during the genocide], he told me that he would kill me. He worked at a roadblock during the genocide. But no one has accused him yet. When I realized I was pregnant, I thought that I had to accept it because

it came from God. Now I am the only Tutsi living here. Once I fled to Gikongoro, but he followed me there and brought me back. Maybe he loves me or he would not have followed me. As long as he does not want to kill me, I will stay with him because I could not find another husband. His brother tells him that he should not live with a Tutsi—that he should kill me. But he said he would not. I do not think that he wants to kill me anymore. My mother-in-law lives with us. She always tells me "You Tutsi girls, you are too proud." I must accept him—God sent him.[89]

Monique is a Hutu woman who was nineteen years old when the fighting began. She was taken as a "wife" by a soldier with the Armed Forces and kept in a forced "marriage." At the end of the genocide, he took her with him to Zaire when he fled. She stayed there for a few months. During that time, she became pregnant. Since the soldier decided to return to Rwanda, he was put into an army reintegration camp in Rubona in Butare prefecture. Monique was housed with the wives of other reintegrated soldiers. "Because my husband had protected me during the war, it was accepted that I would come to his house," she said. Today, Monique is living alone in his house with the baby, while her "husband" is in the retraining camp. She has taken the baby to see her family, but has never taken the baby to his family.[90]

Rape and Mutilation

Often the rape of women was accompanied or followed by mutilation of the sexual organs or of features held to be characteristic of the Tutsi ethnic group. Sexual mutilations included the pouring of boiling water into the vagina; the opening of the womb to cut out an unborn child before killing the mother; cutting off breasts; slashing the pelvis area; and the mutilation of vaginas.[91] One doctor treated a young woman about twenty-one years old who had been permanently

---

[89]Human Rights Watch/FIDH interview, Rusatira commune, Butare prefecture, March 23, 1996.

[90]Human Rights Watch/FIDH interview, Kigali, March 16, 1996.

[91]Coordination of Women's Advocacy, "Mission on Gender-Based War Crimes Against Women and Girls During the Genocide in Rwanda: Summary of Findings and Recommendations," p. 7.

mutilated after acid was thrown on her vagina and who had to be sent to Belgium for reconstructive surgery. The woman had subsequently tested HIV positive.[92] Assailants mutilated features considered "Tutsi," including thin noses and long fingers. A number of victims had two or three fingers or parts of fingers chopped off. Even when victims had joints damaged rather than actually severed, they will probably be permanently disabled because joints are difficult to repair. The Director of Kigali Central Hospital noted that they had treated a number of cases of women with facial scars, blinded by gunshots or deliberate mutilation, as well as mutilated vaginas, fingers, noses and breasts. In one case, they treated a twenty-two year old woman who had been dumped in a ditch and set on fire after being doused with petrol.[93]

One twenty-five-year-old woman, **Denise**, had been married for two months when the militia came to her house on April 20, 1994. People had warned them that the militia were coming, so her husband jumped out of the window. She stayed, thinking that they would not harm her. About six militia came into the house with machetes and torches. She recognized some of them as neighbors. They dragged her outside, and started demanding where her husband was. She recounted what happened:

> When I refused to answer, they began to beat me on the legs with sticks. Then one of them raped me. He said, "you are lucky. Your god is still with you because we don't want to kill you. Now the Hutu have won. You Tutsi, we are going to exterminate you. You won't own anything." When he finished, he took me inside and put me on a bed. He held one leg of mine open and another one held the other leg. He called everyone who was outside and said, "you come and see how Tutsikazi are on the inside." Then he said, "You Tutsikazi, you think you are the only beautiful women in the world." Then he cut out the inside of my vagina. He took the flesh outside, took a small stick and put what he had cut on the top. He stuck the stick in the ground outside the door and was shouting, "Everyone who comes past here will see how Tutsikazi look." Then he came

[92]Human Rights Watch/FIDH interview, Dr. Gladstone Habimana, director, Maternity ward, Kigali Central Hospital, Kigali, March 18, 1996.

[93]Human Rights Watch/FIDH interview, Dr. Emile Rwamasirabo, director, Kigali Central Hospital, Kigali, March 16, 1996.

back inside and beat me again. Up to today, my legs are swollen. Then they left. I crawled out of the house bleeding. There was blood everywhere. A Hutu neighbor took me and put traditional medicine on me. I stayed for over a month with her until I could walk. During that time, she hid me and helped me. When the militias found out where I was, I had to leave again. I fled to another neighbor. In July 1994, the RPF came. I still have medical problems. I have extreme pain every month during my menstrual period. I have not seen a doctor. I have heard of the International Criminal Tribunal and I would talk to them, but they have never come here. I reported my case to the authorities three times, but nothing has happened.[94]

On March 30, 1996, a British Broadcasting Company (BBC) news program announced that Rwandan authorities had arrested a journalist named Joseph Ruyenzi of Radio Rwanda and had charged him with having raped and mutilated Denise. The broadcast said that he had been previously summoned three times and had ignored the summons. Ruyenzi, who is being held in Kigali Central prison, has apparently protested his innocence and others have declared that he has been arrested for purely political reasons.

Jane had witnessed the rape, mutilation and killing of women who were speared through their vaginas:

I was at my house with my aunt and her five children when a group of Interahamwe came shouting and making noise. We tried to escape. Everywhere, people were being killed. I was caught by a group of Interahamwe on April 11, 1994, along with about twenty other women and we were held by them in Gatare sector. Some of them decided to rape us before killing us. Others of them refused to rape us. The ones that wanted to rape us began to rape the women one by one. About ten of them would gang-rape a woman, and when they had finished, they would kill her by pushing a sharpened stick the size of a broomstick into her vagina until she was bleeding and almost dead. I saw them do this to several women. All the time, they were saying things like "we want to have a taste of Tutsi

---

[94]Human Rights Watch/FIDH interview, Kayenzi commune, Gitarama prefecture, March 26, 1996.

women." One of them told us that they were going to chop the Tutsi women into pieces over days—one leg today, another arm tomorrow—until we died slowly. I managed to escape from them while they were raping and hid in the bushes until May 2 when the RPF saved us.[95]

Rape of Hutu Women

Although most rapes were perpetrated against Tutsi women, a number of Hutu women were raped during the genocide.[96] In some cases, Hutu women married to Tutsi men were targeted.

Christine is a Hutu woman who was married to a Tutsi man. When the killings began, twenty-five-year-old Christine and her family sought refuge at the home of Cyrille Ruvugama, a member of parliament who has since fled to Zaire. On May 5, 1994, the militia came to the grounds of the house. Two of the militia raped her, while the others stood around looking. She recognized one of the militia who was wearing banana leaves. Christine said:

> They said "we want to know what Tutsi vaginas are like. If you refuse, we will kill you." They did not know I was a Hutu; my husband was Tutsi. I gave myself so I would not be killed, and to save my children [two years old and four months old], but they killed the children anyway after they raped me.

The militia then proceeded to kill Christine's husband and threatened Christine with a spear, telling her to accept them. She recognized one of the men. Following the genocide, she went to the commune office and reported the man for killing her husband and children and for raping her. The accused is now in Gitarama prison. The other militiaman who raped her has been accused of killing by others and is being held in a police lock-up. When Christine went to report the second man, she went with another woman who had witnessed what had happened. She said, "if it

---

[95]Human Rights Watch/FIDH interview, Nyarugenge commune, Kigali prefecture, April 8, 1996.

[96]Some Hutu women also participated in the genocide and encouraged the killing and rape of Tutsi women. See African Rights, *Rwanda: Not So Innocent: When Women Become Killers*, (London: African Rights, 1995).

had been a woman [investigator], I would have told her everything. I could not tell a military man everything that had happened to me."[97]

Claudine is another Hutu woman who was married to a Tutsi man. When the war began, she and her husband were living in Kanzenze commune, Kigali prefecture, with their five children. At the time, she was thirty years old and seven months pregnant. She said:

> My husband was in Kigali the day the war broke out and they started the killings. I stayed in my house because I was too pregnant to run. They came and killed my children. After they took my children, I went into labor and later my baby was born dead. The next day, I went out to find the bodies of my children. I saw an Interahamwe there taking the clothes of the dead people lying on the ground. He grabbed me and cut me with a knife on the arms and legs. I begged him to kill me. He raped me and then left me thinking I was dead. After a few days, I crawled to a sugar-cane plantation and stayed there in hiding. One day, I saw a group of people. I went to them. I did not care who they were or if they killed me. They were the RPF. They took me to Gitarama. There were many others like me who were raped during the genocide.[98]

Other Hutu women were targeted because they tried to protect Tutsi:

Rose, a twenty-eight-year-old woman, was raped after being accused of hiding Tutsi. Today, she has a child from the rape. She said:

> I am a Hutu woman. During the genocide, three of my Tutsi friends came to hide in my house. I was living with my family because I was not married. In the middle of April, the Interahamwe came to our house and asked for all the Tutsi. We denied that there were any Tutsi. The first time they left without doing anything. They came back a second time, and said that

---

[97]Human Rights Watch/FIDH interview, Taba commune, Gitarama prefecture, April 3, 1996.

[98]Human Rights Watch/FIDH interview, Kanzenze commune, Kigali prefecture, March 28, 1996.

they knew that I was hiding Tutsi. They searched the house, but could not find anyone so they accused me of letting them get away. They threatened to kill me for hiding Tutsi. One of the Interahamwe, Nzabonimana David—about 50 years old; he was killed by the RPA later—asked me for money. I told him that I didn't have any. He told me that I was going to die because I had hidden people and now was not prepared to pay. He put a long knife at my throat and told me that he was going to kill me the way he wanted to. He took me out to the coffee bushes and pushed me on the ground and raped me. After he raped me, he told the other Interahamwe that I was useless and could not give them any money. He also told the others not to rape me because I might have AIDS and could contaminate them. I think he told them that to defend me from being raped by the others. After the Interahamwe left, I tried to go home. I was not badly wounded, but I was hurt and could not walk properly. I still wonder, even today, if I have been given AIDS. I have never seen a doctor because I have no money.[99]

Maria is a young Hutu woman who was a student in Gikongoro before the genocide. Two years later, she is still so traumatized from her experience that she cannot look up when recounting what happened to her. According to the medical personnel who treat her, Maria continues to suffer hallucinations and frequently has weeping fits. She does not like to see or to be near men. On April 15, 1994, the Interahamwe came and killed her grandparents, her two aunts and her brother. As she was fleeing, she was caught by five militia who raped her.

Following the rape, eighteen-year-old Maria's vagina was severely slashed with knives by the militia who shouted "we are going to kill you so you will want death. When the RPF comes, there will be no one left alive." She knew one of the men. The next day, Maria was found by a Red Cross team who transported her to a hospital. The rape and mutilation had resulted in extensive damage to her vaginal area. She was taken to Kigali Central Hospital where a doctor who remained on duty performed surgery, amid the pandemonium caused by the killings. She was hemorrhaging because the mutilation had destroyed the wall between her vagina and rectum. She stayed in the hospital until July 1994 when the RPF came. In January 1995, Maria was sent to Belgium for reconstructive surgery. At that time,

---

[99]Human Rights Watch/FIDH interview, Taba commune, Gitarama prefecture, April 9, 1996.

the doctors who treated Maria discovered that an infection had spread to her uterus and a hysterectomy had to be performed immediately. The doctors also found that the rectal/vaginal wall and the anal sphincter had been irreparably damaged. They attempted as best as possible to perform reconstructive surgery, but Maria will never be able to be sexually active for the rest of her life. The doctors also discovered that she is carrying the AIDS virus.

"What has happened has happened," Maria said, "Now the question is how to survive. They have ruined my future." She continued, "I hope God will punish them. I am not the only one. What they did to me they did to many others. But what can I do?" Maria's one wish is to continue attending school to complete her studies. However, she had no money to pay school fees.

ONGOING PROBLEMS FACING RWANDAN WOMEN

As a result both of the violence inflicted upon them and of their second class status in society, female survivors in Rwanda continue to be faced with overwhelming problems. Many women who lost everything and are heads of households for the first time are faced with the difficult responsibility of trying to rebuild their lives while providing food, shelter and school fees for themselves and their surviving relatives. Among other things, Rwandan rape survivors have had to deal with the social isolation and ostracization experienced by rape victims worldwide, severe health complications, and the children born of rape. In addition, many widows have been unable to return to their property because of discrimination under customary law which does not give them the right to inherit. The lack of judicial accountability for the perpetrators of the genocide is further intensifying the victims' physical and psychological trauma.

There is a strong sentiment on the part of a broad spectrum of Rwandan women that the Rwandan government and the international community are not adequately addressing the overwhelming problems that women currently face. Regardless of their status—Tutsi, Hutu, displaced, returnees—all are facing problems because of the upheaval caused by the genocide and aggravated by their generally disadvantaged status as women. One women's rights activist, Judith Kanakuzu, the director of Duterimbere, a Kigali-based credit union for women said: "We must look for solutions together. Everyone has problems, not just the rape victims. Take the displaced woman who does not know how to get back home. Or the woman whose husband was killed and has her own children and her brother's orphans to raise. Or the woman whose husband is in prison. The consequences of the genocide are being carried on the backs of women."[100] "You do not know the kind of suffering that women are carrying around inside them," said Marie-Claire Mukasine, a lawyer who worked at Hagaruka, a Kigali-based legal advice center for women. "If someone does not do something, they are going to explode."[101]

Virtually every woman interviewed by Human Rights Watch/FIDH noted the fact that while women make up some 70 percent of the population, government policies and international aid programs have not allocated adequate resources to

---

[100]Human Rights Watch/FIDH interview, Judith Kanakuzu, director general, Duterimbere, Kigali, March 19, 1996.

[101]Human Rights Watch/FIDH interview, Marie-Claire Mukasine, coordinator, Hagaruka, Kigali, March 20, 1996.

deal with the particular problems facing Rwandan women. Time and again, women pointed to the current problems that they are facing: poverty, homelessness, inadequate health care, the desolate isolation of being a widow or a rape victim or both in a society that values women primarily as wives and mothers, and the problem of children from rape. Women interviewed were often trying unsuccessfully to obtain access to their husband's property, pension or bank account. "Someone once told me that it is better to live through a war than after a war," said one woman survivor. "I understand that now."

Often, the lack of an adequate international or national response to their needs was compared by women to the rapid response of the international community to other needy groups, such as Rwandan prisoners held in dismal conditions, or food relief and other services provided to refugees in Zaire and Tanzania. Many women survivors are angry that the abuses against them are not being adequately addressed. Annunciata Nyiratamba with the Association for Widows of the April Genocide (AVEGA) said:

> Women are alone. They have lost everything. But there are no
> programs for them. No-one speaks about the survivors. No one
> talks about their problems. We are watching what the world will
> do for the survivors and what it does for the returnees and the
> refugees. This is a problem for reconciliation. There needs to
> be assistance for victims, not just for refugees, prisons and
> returnees. It's unbalanced. Concretely, there is nothing for the
> women and yet they constitute the bulk of the survivors."[102]

Another genocide survivor stressed that in many cases, women are just trying to get access to things that they are entitled to, such as their property: "The new government is not doing enough for women. We need a policy for widows and their children. Many women can't get their money or their property back. We're not begging. We just want our rights recognized."[103]

Others expressed dismay at the fact that they were being urged to forget what happened to them in the name of peace and reconciliation. Women want

---

[102]Human Rights Watch/FIDH interview, Annunciata Nyiratamba, Association for Widows of the April Genocide (AVEGA), Kigali, March 19, 1996.

[103]Human Rights Watch/FIDH interview, Ester Mujawayo, Association for Widows of the April Genocide (AVEGA), Kigali, March 18, 1996.

justice. It is important to them that the perpetrators of the violence against them are held accountable. As one widow put it:

> People are forgetting. They only want to take the present and not deal with the past. People say that the genocide is too big. So, let us find huge means to deal with it, not minimize it. We are living with our past. We don't want to allow people to just forget it. We are widows like other widows, but we have things that are particular to our group. Our situation is different. Many of us never found the bodies of our husbands or children. We have never buried them. We have never mourned them. There has been no funeral. We are left wondering about his last moments. How was he killed? Was he hacked to death? Was he shot? Was he killed by machete? How long did he lie on the road? Was he eaten by dogs? This isn't like a regular widow. Other widows don't have this torment. Other widows still have the rest of their family, the other relatives. Most of us have no other family. We are the sole survivors. And this was done within neighborhoods. What's left is mistrust. Families of those who killed your family are still there. We don't have houses any more. There isn't even anywhere for us to return to cry. Everything has been destroyed. You can't describe us in banal terms and say we are widows like any other widows. It's very difficult and very different.[104]

An important development in Rwanda is the growing number of women's organizations emerging to deal with the broad spectrum of issues facing women. Rwandan women have organized themselves to provide trauma counseling groups, credit unions, legal advice centers, housing construction groups, survivor support groups, medical centers and other services. While these efforts do receive some financial and political support from the international community and the Rwandan government, they should receive greater support. The relevant government ministries and international donors must consult and cooperate more closely with these women's organizations to support and enhance their programs.

---

[104]Ibid.

Stigma, Isolation and Ostracization

As elsewhere in the world, rape and other sex-based violations against women carry a stigma in Rwanda. Many of the Rwandan women who have been raped do not dare reveal publicly that they have been raped. Women who acknowledge being raped fear that they will be marked as rape victims and may be ostracized by their families and community. Women know that integrating into their communities and resuming their lives will be more difficult if their rape is known. As a result, many women survivors of sexual violence are reluctant to seek medical assistance or to report what happened to them. "The women who have had children after being raped are the most marginalized," said social worker Godelieva Mukasarasi. "People say that this is the child of an Interahamwe."[105]

Rape survivors also expressed concern that they would never be able to remarry. Many Rwandans seem to assume that rape victims have a sexually transmitted disease, most often AIDS, and rape victims fear that they will never get a husband if they admit they were raped. In Rwandan society, where women are valued primarily for their role as wives and mothers, the issue of marriageability is extremely important. Further, for many women, marriage is their best option to obtain economic security and some protection. "It's always sad to see a girl who survived [the genocide]," said Jeanne, herself a rape survivor. "They have no future. Some marry without really wanting to, because they are all alone. They can't farm their parents' land— they need a husband to help work the fields."[106]

The silence surrounding rape affects women in myriad ways, but particularly with respect to their sexual and reproductive health. Many women who have been raped or mutilated continue to suffer health problems, but have not consulted a doctor because of the stigma attached and the cost and inaccessibility of health care. Dr. Rwamasirabo, the director of Kigali Central Hospital, noted that rape victims were reluctant to come forward to seek medical treatment because of the fear of being judged because "society is looking at you" and because of the shame of being raped.[107] Even women who have sought medical treatment often have not disclosed to their doctor the fact that they were raped. Dr. Odette

---

[105]Human Rights Watch/FIDH interview, Godelieva Mukasarasi, coordinator SEVOFA, Réseau des femmes, Taba, March 26, 1996.

[106]Human Rights Watch/FIDH interview, Birenga Commune, Kibungo prefecture, March 31, 1996.

[107]Human Rights Watch/FIDH interview, Dr. Emile Rwamasirabo, director, Kigali Central Hospital, Kigali, March 16, 1996.

Nyiramilimo of Le Bon Samaritain Clinic noted that most raped women coming in for treatment would not say that they had been raped: "They would usually say something like 'I have had sex with someone I don't know.'" Then later on in the conversation, I start asking questions such as "how many were there?" to elicit information about what had happened."[108] Dr. Etienne Mubarutso, a gynecologist at University Hospital in Butare, who has examined hundreds of rape victims since the genocide, described his experience with rape cases:

> It has been two years since the war, but these patients are very difficult to cure. Initially, they come in with infections, vaginal infections, urinary tract problems—problems that are sexually transmitted. You cure the direct illness, but psychologically, they are not healed. They continue to come back complaining of cramps or pains, but there is nothing physically wrong with them. These women are profoundly marked psychologically. Medically, they are healed, but they continue to be sick. And there are no services that specifically deal with the problems these women have. There are some groups for widows, and the like, but there are no groups to help women who have gone through this [rape].[109]

Psychologically, women feel isolated. Along with that, many expressed strong feelings of loneliness and despair. One widow said:

> It is as if we are now beginning a new life. Our past is so sad. We are not understood by society . . . We are not protected against anything. Widows are without families, without houses, without money. We become crazy. We aggravate people with our problems. We are the living dead.[110]

---

[108]Human Rights Watch/FIDH interview, Dr. Odette Nyiramilimo, Le Bon Samaritain Clinic, Kigali, March 18, 1996.

[109]Human Rights Watch/FIDH interview, Dr. Etienne Mubarutso, gynecologist, University Hospital, Butare, March 27, 1996.

[110]Human Rights Watch/FIDH interview, member, Association des femmes chefs de families, Kigali, March 28, 1996.

Some women spoke about the fact that now as single women, they no longer have any status in society:

> In the past, there was respect for widows. Now there is nothing.
> You are nothing if you are a widow now. We have always been
> considered lower than a man. But now as a woman without a
> husband, a brother, a father or an uncle, you are nothing. The
> widows are isolated by the community. You don't get invited to
> community events. People forget to invite you to weddings.
> People forget you. You are alone. It's a feeling of being really
> isolated.[111]

The accusations of collaboration by the returnees against survivors further shames and isolates these women. Women survivors often feel guilty for having survived. One woman said, "It is assumed that most survivors were raped, that if you survived, you were raped . . . [the returnees] say, how did you survive? Women often feel guilty for surviving. They feel responsible."[112]

Hutu widows also suffer from isolation. Those whose husbands were Tutsi often are rejected by their husbands' families, who may blame them for their sons deaths, and by Tutsi widows who distrust them because they are Hutu. Many of these widows, as well as those whose husbands were political moderates, hesitate to return to their own families or to associate with other Hutu in the community because they hold them responsible for the genocide and even for the killings of their husbands and children. One Hutu widow who lost her Tutsi husband and her four sons (only her twenty-year-old daughter who was held by an Interahamwe for rape survived) said:

> Two of the militia who killed my family are now in prison and
> three others have gone to Burundi and Kigali, I think. One was
> killed. It is not easy to live with the Hutu women in this area
> now. Even though I am Hutu, I still cannot live with them after
> what they have done. I am staying with my neighbors. I cannot
> even go back to my house. It is destroyed. We are living as if
> we are dead. When they kill your husband and children and then

---

[111]Human Rights Watch/FIDH interview, Ester Mujawayo, Association for Widows of the April Genocide (AVEGA), Kigali, March 18, 1996.

[112]Ibid.

leave you, it is like killing you. They left us to die slowly. I wish every day that I was dead.[113]

Women are also trying to combat the isolation and break the silence. "Many women begged to be killed during the genocide," said Ester Mujawayo of the Association for Widows of the April Genocide, "They were refused and told 'you will die of sadness.'" We want to challenge the [the rapists/killers] and live. We don't want to remain the living dead."[114] Widows associations and trauma groups for women do exist and women are coming together to begin to deal with their losses and injuries. Some women are talking about their experiences of sexual violence, others are beginning to rebuild homes, others are forming trauma groups. Women's organizations are beginning to organize and empower women and it is these emergent efforts that the Rwandan government and the international community must support.

Health

The health consequences of gender-based violence against women often continue long after the abuse. As mentioned above, women frequently did not seek medical assistance because of the stigma attached to sexual violence, a lack of money or the inaccessibility of health care centers. These difficulties cause rape-related health problems to worsen. Some women chose not to visit a doctor because of the fear of discovering that they carry the AIDS virus.

Rwandan doctors note that the most common medical problems were sexually transmitted diseases, such as syphilis, gonorrhea or vaginitis. Other medical problems include AIDS, vesico-vaginal fistula, trauma, mutilation, complications from botched abortions and psychological problems.

Among young girls, pregnancies and childbirth pose a great health risk to the mother. Health professionals noted complications arising from young girls giving birth including vesico-vaginal or recto-vagina fistula and future complications including uterine problems and scarring of the vaginal tissue affecting their ability to have a normal sex life or to give birth in the future. Some

---

[113]Human Rights Watch/FIDH interview, Rusatira commune, Butare prefecture, March 23, 1996.

[114]Human Rights Watch/FIDH interview, Ester Mujawayo, Association for Widows of the April Genocide (AVEGA), March 18, 1996.

of these young girls have lost hope that they would be married and have more children in the future.[115]

It is impossible to reach any firm conclusions about the transmission of AIDS during the genocide because of the difficulty of ascertaining when a given individual was exposed to the virus.[116] Nonetheless, it is certain that some women were infected with the virus as a result of being raped. The rate of HIV infection in Rwanda was extremely high before the genocide: an estimated 25 percent of the population and an estimated 35 percent in the Rwandan army were HIV positive.[117] The Director of Kigali Central Hospital reported that he had examined two sisters, ages two and fourteen years at Kigali Central Hospital in December 1995. Both girls had been raped during the genocide. Both had contracted chronic vaginitis and the fourteen year-old had also contracted the HIV virus. He believes that the girl almost certainly contracted the virus through rape.[118]   The Rwandan government asserts:

> Without question, the situation of HIV/AIDS infection was aggravated considerably between April and July 1994. A large number of girls and women who survived the genocide were

---

[115]Bonnet, "Le viol des femmes survivantes du génocide du Rwanda," p. 24.

[116]A May 1995 study of 500 pregnant women who had come in for pre-natal counseling was conducted at Kigali Central Hospital. Of the group, 25 percent tested HIV positive—the same rate as before the war. Sixty percent of this sample were living in Kigali before the war and 40 percent abroad. Of the 127 women who tested HIV positive, ninety-six of them had been living abroad before the war. This study underscores the difficulty of making any firm conclusions about the transmission of AIDS during the genocide. Human Rights Watch/FIDH interview, Dr. Emile Rwamasirabo, director, Kigali Central Hospital, Kigali, March 16, 1996.

[117]AIDS has become the third most-common cause of death in Rwanda. In 1993, it was estimated that 150,000 to 200,000 people were infected. In December 1992, the percentage of infection among pregnant women in Kigali was estimated at 8.5 percent. In the rural areas, it was estimated to be 2.2 percent. In Kigali, among patients with sexually transmitted diseases, the percentage that tested positive for the HIV virus which causes AIDS was 73 percent among women and 55 percent among men. Government of Rwanda, *Rapport National*, p. 58.

[118]Human Rights Watch/FIDH interview, Dr. Emile Rwamasirabo, director, Kigali Central Hospital, Kigali, March 16, 1996.

raped; others are living in displaced persons camps or refugee camps, where the conditions of hygiene and promiscuity favor the transmission of HIV/AIDS.[119]

An AIDS awareness center based in Kigali asserts that the national percentage of HIV carriers has remained the same since the genocide—25 percent. The director, Janvière Mukantwali, noted that a large influx of returnees came from Burundi, Zaire and Uganda—all high-risk countries for the HIV virus, and this population has contributed to keeping the percentage the same despite the widespread killings of the genocide. She also noted that "since the genocide, people have become fatalistic about death and are not protecting themselves from AIDS because they believe that it is just another death like any other death." After the genocide, the Center established an AIDS focus group for women. They discovered, to their surprise, that rates of sexual activity outside of marriage appeared, as far as they could ascertain, to be notably higher among women since the genocide, in large part because women were looking for "affection and protection." However, despite the rise in sexual activity, women were not protecting themselves from AIDS.[120]

Although abortion is illegal in Rwanda, many women could not bear the thought of having a child from the Interahamwe who had raped them.[121] Some of the women who became pregnant after being raped had self-induced abortions, often at great risk to their health, particularly in the late stages of pregnancy. Others were able to obtain abortions in neighboring Zaire or in private clinics in

------

[119]Government of Rwanda, *Rapport National*, p. 59.

[120]Human Rights Watch/FIDH interview, Janvière Mukantwali, *Centre d'Information de Documentation et de Counseling sur le SIDA* (CIDC), Kigali, April 12, 1996.

[121]Article 325 of the Rwanda Penal Code states: "Anyone who, using food, drink, medicine, manoeuvres, violence or any other means, intentionally performs an abortion on a pregnant woman who has not given her consent, will be punished with imprisonment for five to ten years. If the woman consented, the guilty party will be punished with imprisonment for two to five years. The woman who voluntarily allows or attempts to perform an abortion or who consents to the use of means administered for that purpose will be punished with imprisonment for two to five years." Delphine Tailfer, *Les Droits de la Femme dans la Legislation Rwandaise et la Convention des Nations Unies sur L'Elimination de Toutes les Formes de Discrimination a l'egard des Femmes: Propositions de Révision Légale*, (Kigali: Ministère de la Famille et de la Promotion de la Femme/UNICEF), p. 145.

Rwanda if they could afford to do so. The current Rwandan government has not legalized abortion, perhaps in part because Roman Catholics—the leading religious group in the country—reject the practice, and in part because traditional beliefs oppose it. A February 1995 study by the Ministry of Family and the Promotion of Women found that of 716 rape cases, 472 women had become pregnant and 282 had aborted.[122] Others did not know how to abort and many did not want to for religious or social reasons. For others, the pregnancy was too far along to consider abortion. Doctors treated a number of pregnant rape victims with complications arising from self-induced or clandestine abortions. Many of these abortions had been carried out in the third trimester at great risk to the woman's life. Some women had been bleeding for up to three months before they sought medical treatment.[123] The Director of Kigali Central Hospital noted that some of these self-induced abortions had caused uterine infections, rupturing of the uterus, hemorrhaging, and other gynecological complications. He added, "It is difficult to know what they had used, and since abortion is illegal, the hospital could not offer abortion as a medical service. But it is not just that it is illegal, the religious and social mores also disapprove of abortion and so it is not commonly practiced."[124]

The Director of Kigali Central Hospital also noted that the disfigurements caused by mutilations seem to have affected female victims more than male victims because women are often valued for their beauty. He said:

> Women often come in to see what can be done to make them look whole. Even if a prosthetic will not be of any practical use, they want it so they can have the appearance of a whole hand or foot. In other cases, the disfiguring across the face makes it impossible to do anything. Often the type of reconstructive surgery required needs highly skilled doctors and they are not available here."[125]

---

[122]Government of Rwanda, *Rapport National*, p. 72.

[123]Human Rights Watch/FIDH interview, Dr. Gladstone Habimana, director, Maternity ward, Kigali Central Hospital, Kigali, March 18, 1996.

[124]Human Rights Watch/FIDH interview, Dr. Emile Rwamasirabo, director, Kigali Central Hospital, Kigali, March 16, 1996.

[125]Ibid.

Children from Rape

Many of the numerous rapes during the genocide resulted in what were called "pregnancies of war." According to estimates of the National Population Office, survivors of rape have given birth to between 2,000 and 5,000 children who are known as "enfants non-desirés" (unwanted children) or "enfants de mauvais souvenir" (children of bad memories), or "children of hate." Health workers at Kigali and Kabgayi hospitals had noted that after September 1994, over half the pregnant women seen for consultations had been raped: between six to seven out of ten each day.[126] In the survey of 304 rape survivors conducted by the Ministry of Family and Promotion of Women in collaboration with UNICEF, 35 percent had become pregnant after being raped.[127]

The response of women to these children has been mixed. Understandably, many women were not able to accept the child because they associated the child with the brutality perpetrated upon them and their families by the rapist. "How can you have a child of someone who killed your husband and children?" asked one Rwandan woman.[128] One study of rape in Rwanda, by Dr. Catherine Bonnet, noted:

> The psychopathy of pregnancies resulting from rape in Rwanda is the same as that which has been observed in France and in the former Yugoslavia: these pregnancies are rejected and concealed, often denied and discovered late. They are often accompanied by attempted self-induced abortions or violent fantasies against the child; indeed, even infanticide. Suicidal ideas are frequently present. Some women probably committed suicide without revealing the reason when they discovered that they had become pregnant by their rapist-tormentor.[129]

Dr. Odette Nyiramilimo noted from her experience that:

---

[126]Bonnet, "Le viol des femmes survivantes du génocide du Rwanda,", p. 23.

[127]Government of Rwanda, Ministry of Family and the Promotion of Women, "Enquête effectuée auprès des victimes."

[128]Human Rights Watch/FIDH interview, Hutu woman working in a nongovernmental organization, Kigali, March 18, 1996.

[129]Bonnet, "Le viol des femmes survivantes du génocide du Rwanda," p. 22.

Women would come in and say that they didn't want the child. Others decided to have the child and didn't say anything about the rape, but then during the delivery, they would cry out things like, "my child is an Interahamwe!" Some didn't even want to see their babies at first, and only later did they accept them.[130]

Often, women refused to register themselves by name at the hospital, preferring to remain anonymous. Some then abandoned their babies at the hospital two or three days after delivering. Many asked for a doctor of the same ethnicity as themselves.[131] One woman handed over her baby to the Ministry of Family and the Promotion of Women, saying "this is a child of the state." Health professionals assume that a number of women gave birth in secret and later committed infanticide. They also believe that a number of women who gave birth in the hospital allowed their babies to die after returning home. Health professionals described cases where even women who had decided to keep their babies took one look at the child in the delivery room, saw what they believed to be a resemblance to the rapist, and rejected the baby.

Other women decided to accept their child. In some families, the mother's decision to keep the child has caused deep divisions in the family. In others, the child is being raised normally within the community. Women spoke of the difficulties they were having:

Marcelline, a thirty-seven year old rape survivor was one of those who decided to keep her baby. She was raped by an Interahamwe in Musambira commune during the genocide. He threw her on the ground and said "I must rape you or kill you." After raping her, he took her money and left her naked. She said, "I didn't even want to open my eyes. There were bodies everywhere." When she realized that she was pregnant, she did not care because she believed that she would be killed sooner or later. However, having survived the genocide, she accepted the baby girl. "The child is innocent. She knows nothing. She has a right to live,"

---

[130]Human Rights Watch/FIDH interview, Dr. Nyiramilimo Odette, Le Bon Samaritain Clinic, Kigali, March 18, 1996.

[131]Bonnet, "Le viol des femmes survivantes du génocide du Rwanda," p. 18.

Marcelline explained. "But no one knows that she is a child of an Interahamwe. No one talks about what happened."[132]

Alphonsine was nineteen years old and living with her grandparents in Taba commune when the Interahamwe attacked them on April 12, 1994. She escaped through a window at the back, but was caught by one Interahamwe. She said:

> He told me that he knew that even through I was Hutu that my grandparents were Tutsi (my mother is Tutsi) and that he would kill them if I did not submit to him. He took me to the sorghum field and raped me on the ground there. Before he left, he asked me to tell him where we kept all our money. After they left, I escaped to my parents' house. I never saw a doctor after the rape, but a few months later, I realized I was pregnant. I was angry about the pregnancy and even thought about getting an abortion, but I had no money and no way to do it. I gave birth to twins in January 1995. At the time, I accepted them. I could not think about killing them. They survived for eleven months, but died. When I took them to the hospital, they couldn't find anything wrong . . . My family knew that I had children of an Interahamwe. They all accepted it, but sometimes my mother would complain about the children and say that they were not children of this family. Sometimes when they cried, my mother would tell me to stop the noise or to give these children back to their father. I still think a lot about the rape. I wonder if I have AIDS.[133]

Another case involved **Francine**, a thirteen year old girl whose family was killed before she was abducted to Zaire by an Interahamwe for four months. She managed to return to Kigali in December 1995 and located her aunt. Francine denied that she had been sexually abused at all, but shortly afterwards it became clear that she was pregnant. A cousin in the family wanted Francine to have an abortion, but her aunt, a devout Catholic, locked the young girl in a room until she

---

[132]Human Rights Watch/FIDH interview, Taba commune, Gitarama prefecture, March 26, 1996.

[133]Human Rights Watch/FIDH interview, Taba commune, Gitarama prefecture, April 9, 1996.

delivered to ensure that the nephew would not take her for an abortion. Francine now has a baby, and the cousin refuses to visit his mother any longer. Another case involved a twenty-two year old woman who decided to keep a child from rape in opposition to the wishes of her family who named the child "child of hate." The mother later renamed the child.[134]

Rose, a Hutu woman whose rape testimony was included above, described her response to being pregnant:

> Later, I found out that I was pregnant and I was unhappy. I thought about having an abortion, but I was afraid of dying. I knew that I was going to have an unwanted child and that I was not able to look after a baby. But I didn't want to behave like an Interahamwe and abandon my baby. So, I have kept my baby. He is now one year and four months. Almost all my family members have refused to accept the baby—it is a child of an Interahamwe. They have told me that they do not want a child of wicked people. They always tell me that when my baby grows up that they will not give him a parcel of land. I don't know what is going to happen to him. The only help I have received is from Réseau des Femmes [a local women's rights organization]."[135]

Children born out of wedlock before the genocide faced some stigma, but generally found a place in their mothers' families. No can predict, however, how children born of rape during the genocide will be treated as they grow up. "It is the unbearable question," said one Rwandan woman who works with a church organization, "Can we ever tell these unwanted children? Will they ever know the truth? What will be the reaction of this child when he learns the truth? What should the government be doing?"[136]

---

[134]Human Rights Watch/FIDH interview, Godelieva Mukasarasi, coordinator, SEVOFA, *Réseau des femmes*, Taba, March 26, 1996.

[135]Human Rights Watch/FIDH interview, Taba commune, Gitarama prefecture, April 9, 1996.

[136]Human Rights Watch/FIDH interview, Mary Balikungeri, program coordinator, Church World Service, Kigali, March 27, 1996.

Discriminatory Treatment Under the Law

At present, discriminatory civil law provisions which legislate gender inequality remain in effect in violation of the Rwandan constitution and international law.[137] For example, while the 1988 Family Code, which governs marriage, separation and children, recognizes equality of men and women in the household, contradictory provisions in the Family Code declare that the man is the natural head of the household, and that as head of the union, his opinion will prevail. Article 213 of the Family Code also stipulates that a wife cannot engage in commercial activity or employment without authorization from her husband.[138] Under the Penal Code, the punishment prescribed for adultery in the case of women (one month to a year imprisonment) is greater than that for men (one to three months imprisonment).[139] According to the Civil Code, a woman must obtain her husband's authorization for any legal matter in which she must appear in person.[140] The Civil Code also stipulates that a Rwandan woman who marries a non-Rwandan can lose her citizenship. However, a Rwandan man can never lose his citizenship. Similarly, children of a Rwandan man are automatically granted citizenship, while the children of a Rwandan woman married to a non-Rwandan national are not eligible for citizenship unless the father is not known or is stateless.[141]

---

[137]Article 2(1) of the International Covenant on Civil and Political Rights states: "Each State Party to the Covenant undertakes to respect and to ensure to all individuals within its territory and subject to its jurisdiction the rights recognized in this present Covenant, without distinction of any kind, such as race, color, sex, language, religion, political or other opinion, national or social origin, property, birth or other status." Article 26 further provides that all persons are "equal before the law and are entitled without any discrimination to the equal protection of the law."

[138]Government of Rwanda, *Rapport National*, p. 29.

[139]Articles 353-357 of the Rwanda Penal Code. Charles Ntampaka, *La Femme et le mariage* (Kigali: Hagaruka [Association pour la défense des droits de la Femme et de l'Enfant]/United States Embassy, 1993), p. 28.

[140]Government of Rwanda, *Rapport National*, p. 31.

[141]Delphine Tailfer, *Les Droits de la Femme dans la Legislation Rwandaise . . .*, p. 122. See also, Human Rights Watch/Africa/Women's Rights Project, "Botswana: Second Class Citizens, Discrimination Against Women Under Botswana's Citizen Act," *A Human Rights Short Report*, vol. 6, no. 7, September 1994.

Property and Inheritance Rights

As has already been noted in the section on the Status of Rwandan Women, women are extremely disadvantaged and discriminated against under civil and customary law. Since the genocide, this discrimination has been most apparent in the area of property inheritance.

Customary law is generally followed in Rwanda when there is no statutory provision dealing explicitly with the issue, and where the customary practice is not contradictory to the Constitution. However, in practice, customary law which discriminates against women, in violation of the Constitution, continues to be widely applied. Although the Family Code provides statutory direction generally in the area of family law matters, it does not speak directly to the issues of inheritance and succession. Accordingly, customary law is used, even though its application discriminates against women, unless there is a will explicitly designating the beneficiaries. Because customary law designates men as the head of family, they are also recognized to inherit property, name the children, and transmit the family name. Before the genocide, when ethnic affiliation was registered at birth, men transmitted their ethnic identity to their children. In case of the husband's death, the children can be taken from the wife by the man's family because the children "belong" to the husband and his family.

Under customary law, women do not inherit (and in fact may form part of the husband's "belongings" subject to inheritance). Upon the death of the husband, the eldest son becomes the head of the family or the husband's family claims the inheritance.[142] Traditionally, girls cannot inherit from their father nor from other members of the family, unless they are unmarried and there is either no male successor or the male successor is not traceable.[143] There have been court decisions which recognize the right of unmarried daughters to inherit in the absence of a male child. In cases where a son is a minor, the wife must often obtain a declaration from a magistrate in order to administer the inheritance until the son reaches adulthood. Even when women do have recognized rights, they are unlikely to seek the protection of the law either because it is difficult to secure judicial redress or because they are intimidated by the legal process.

---

[142]Human Rights Watch/FIDH interview. Jacque Kabale Nyangezi, lawyer, Ministry of the Family and Promotion of Women. Kigali, March 18, 1996; Ministry of Family and the Promotion of Women. "Rapport de la Commission pour les droits de la Femme," Kigali (undated).

[143]Government of Rwanda, *Rapport National*, p. 31; Ntampaka, *La Femme et la Fille dans leur Famille d'Origine*, pp. 27-28.

Marie-Claire Mukasine of Hagaruka noted that a large number of the cases Hagaruka is dealing with now are in the area of property rights:

> It is a big problem for women in the rural areas. When a married woman tries to get her parents' property, she is told that she has a husband and that she should go to his home. Sometimes the woman herself thinks like that and does not even pursue the property to which she is entitled. Then the surviving male relatives take it. Orphaned children are also having problems getting their parents' land. The property is rightfully theirs, but sometimes conflicts within the family make it difficult. The orphans are usually absorbed by the mother's side of the family. Yet, it is the father's side that wants to take the property (and not always the children).[144]

Another women's rights activist described how these issues are affecting women:

> Women lost their families, their houses, their property—everything. Now they have to raise their surviving children and the children of other dead family and friends . . . Many women who have lost everything have taken in other people's children. But they do not get the property that comes with these children which could help them live . . . They stay in abandoned houses, yet fear putting money into them and then losing it to the former owners. They are often chased from the family property.[145]

Some women survivors of the genocide continue to live with their relatives or friends because they are not able to get access to their property which has been occupied either by families of their husbands or by Rwandan exiles who returned after the genocide.

Hutu widows or Hutu women whose husbands are currently in prison on genocide charges are also vulnerable to being forced off their property. One Hutu

---

[144]Human Rights Watch/FIDH interview, Marie-Claire Mukasine, coordinator, Hagaruka, Kigali, March 20, 1996.

[145]Human Rights Watch/FIDH interview, Bernadette Muhimakazi, Bon Pasteur, Kigali, March 25, 1996.

survivor identified the range of problems that Hutu women are facing in obtaining access to their property:

> Genocide survivors, who are mostly women, are being accused of collaborating by the returnees so the returnees can keep their house. The returnees from Burundi are particularly extremist about blaming all Hutu indiscriminately. Many Hutu women returned to their homes only to find that returnees have occupied their houses. When they try to get their homes back, accusations of collaboration are made against them. Other Hutu women whose husbands are in prison for having participated in the genocide have the same problem. They are being implicated by extension. Hutu survivors are being put in the garbage. There is no place for moderates in this country. I know of cases where the military put a family in someone else's house. You don't dare challenge it. I also know of six people who were imprisoned for trying to get their houses back. One was a woman whose husband is in prison.[146]

Human Rights Watch/FIDH interviewed one Hutu survivor, Thérèse, who had been married to a Tutsi man in Taba commune. Her husband was killed by a number of Interahamwe, some of whom she recognized. They spared her life telling her that they would not kill her because she was a Hutu, but urged her to leave the inyenzi and told her that they could find another husband for her. Thérèse fled to her family and stayed there until the end of the war. When she tried to return to her husband's (and her) home after the genocide, her Tutsi sister-in-law drove her off the property:

> After the war, I went back to my house. My sister-in-law came and told me that she did not want me to live there anymore. My husband's family told me to bring the children and they demanded to know why I was not killed. I kept quiet. My sister-in-law told me not to return and to go marry someone else because they didn't want to live with me. I now live with my family. I went and told the sub-prefect in September 1994 that I was chased from my home. He told me that my sister-in-law

---

[146]Human Rights Watch/FIDH interview, Hutu woman working with an NGO, Kigali, March 18, 1996.

has no right to chase me off my land. So I tried to return. But my sister-in-law has told me that if I come back I will have no peace. I believe her. She accused my three brothers of being Interahamwe, even though they were not, and she had them arrested. They have been held at Gitarama prison since March 1995. I have not tried to go back since because my sister-in-law said that she will get me arrested for taking food to my brothers in prison. I have not gone back to my home because I am afraid for my security. I fear that my sister-in-law will do something to harm me. I know three other cases like this.[147]

On International Women's Day in March 1995, President Pasteur Bizimungu announced that the Ministry of Family and the Promotion of Women would revise the discriminatory laws affecting women and children. The Ministry has begun an extensive legal revision of customary and statutory law which does not comply with the international legal standards. The sub-commission is proposing revisions to discriminatory sections contained in customary law and in the Family Code, the Nationality Code, the Civil Code, the Commercial Code, the Employment Code and the Penal Code.[148] The process has been divided into three phases: (1) meetings of experts to look into discrimination in the law; (2) consultation and education of women; and (3) incorporation of women's suggestions. The first phase began in June 1995 and ended in September 1995. At the time of this writing, the government is in the second phase. However, these efforts, while commendable, have been proceeding slowly and the reforms must be implemented without further delay. The longer the process takes, the less likelihood that women will be able to return to the expropriated land that they seek to reclaim. In the meantime, the government has not put into place interim protections to ensure that women are not forced off their property. Moreover, the government must ensure that the legal reform is actually implemented once the laws are revised and that programs are put into place to redress the effects of discrimination.

---

[147]Human Rights Watch/FIDH interview, Taba commune, Gitarama prefecture, April 3, 1996.

[148]See the section on the status of Rwandan women for a detailed analysis of the discriminatory provisions.

THE NATIONAL AND INTERNATIONAL RESPONSE

Lack of National Judicial Redress

Shortly after assuming power in mid-July 1994, the new government announced its intention to prosecute all those accused of committing crimes during the genocide. But because the former government fled with virtually all the funds and most of the usable equipment belonging to the state, the new government began this effort with few resources to carry out investigations and prosecutions. In addition, many lawyers, judges and prosecutors were killed during the genocide, were themselves implicated in the killings, or fled the country.[149] On the first anniversary of the start of the genocide in April 1995, the Rwandan government brought the first people accused of genocide to court, but their cases were adjourned the same day to permit further investigation and the hearings have not resumed. The government is facing major constraints in attempting to use the national judiciary in order to deal with some 80,000 cases of alleged genocide crimes and is hampered by a lack of human and material resources. The resource issue is accompanied by an apparent lack of political will to begin the trials, and a growing hostility against judicial personnel who pursue investigations too vigorously.[150] Although officials in judicial circles acknowledge that many of the prisoners alleged to have committed genocide crimes are believed to be innocent, it is impossible to refute false accusations before the courts. In some cases, judges and prosecutors who have reviewed cases and ordered releases have been the objects of threats, dismissals, imprisonment or murder.

In the last two years, the Rwandan government has received some U.S. $19 million from Belgium, Canada, Germany, the Netherlands, the United States, and other international donors to help revitalize the judicial system. The government has used the money to pay for buildings and equipment and to train personnel, including police inspectors and magistrates. But even with the addition of these resources, the judicial system remains paralyzed, largely because the government remains divided over how to prosecute and punish those accused of

---

[149]Human Rights Watch/Africa/FIDH, "A New Catastrophe?: Increased International Efforts Required to Punish Genocide and Prevent further Bloodshed," *A Human Rights Short Report,* vol. 6, no. 12, December 1994, p. 12; Human Rights Watch/Africa/FIDH, "Rwanda: The Crisis Continues," *A Human Rights Short Report,* vol. 7, no. 1, April 1995.

[150]Human Rights Watch/Africa/FIDH, press release "New Attacks on Judicial Personnel in Rwanda," May 13, 1996.

cases before the courts. I have not reported my case anywhere
else because I don't have the money to go anywhere else."[154]

Secondly, there is a lack of female judicial investigators. Rape survivors
repeatedly said that if judicial police inspectors were women, they would have
reported the rapes committed against them. Marcelline, who has lived in an
abandoned house since her own home, crops, and cattle were destroyed, said that
she had not reported her rape. The local authorities had asked the community to
go to Gitarama to register the names of all the dead and those who had killed them.
She said that other women were asked about rape, but she had said nothing about
having been raped. "There were no women asking the questions. If it was a
woman, I would have told her," she said, "It is a crime when someone takes you
by force and rapes you. Isn't that a crime?"[155] Another rape survivor said, "if there
were women judges, maybe women would be more willing to go to women about
cases of rape."[156]

Women themselves often do not offer this information easily and, in some
cases, they are unaware that the rape is a prosecutable crime. In other cases,
women remain silent because they fear reprisal from their attacker. One woman,
who witnessed the gang-rape and death of her nineteen-year-old daughter, reported
the killing to the local authorities, but did not mention the rape:

> I lost my daughter in a horrible way. There is nothing I can do,
> there is nothing to believe in now. The man who killed my
> daughter was arrested in November 1995. I tried to find the
> others responsible for killing my family, but they have all left
> the country. I did not mention the rape of my daughter because
> I considered the whole thing as a killing. If rape is by force,
> then it is just like killing. I have never heard of a woman
> accusing someone of rape. I didn't know that rape could be
> prosecuted. I was only asked about the way my daughter was

[154]Human Rights Watch/FIDH interview, Taba commune, Gitarama prefecture,
April 9, 1996.

[155]Human Rights Watch/FIDH interview, Taba commune, Gitarama prefecture,
March 26, 1996.

[156]Human Rights Watch/FIDH interview, Annunciata Nyiratamba, Association for
Widows of the April Genocide (AVEGA), Kigali, March 19, 1996.

genocide. It has continued to arrest hundreds of accused persons every week producing severe overcrowding in prisons and lockups where some 80,000 person await trial. The International Committee of the Red Cross judged the overcrowding so serious and potentially life-threatening that for the first time in its history, provided funds to build new detention facilities. During 1996, several recently trained judicial inspectors and magistrates have been assassinated, and others have encountered opposition from local administrators which has made it impossible for them to function independently or which led to their removal.

According to judicial authorities, prosecutors have prepared over 4,000 cases for trial and some one hundred police inspectors and magistrates are working to investigate others. Few, if any, of the dossiers prepared thus far include charge of rape.[151] Although it is not just victims of rape who are failing to obtain justice women who have been raped face substantial and special problems in pursuit their claims. First, police inspectors are not collecting information on rape in systematic fashion. Deputy Minister of Justice Gerald Gahima told Human Right Watch/FIDH that within the Justice Ministry's investigative teams, "rape has n been receiving the attention it deserves. The main focus has been on the killing and not as many women were killed."[152]

Some judicial investigators are unaware that rape is prosecutabl Inspectors have actually turned away women seeking to report the perpetrators their rape. Rape survivor Ancille said, "In my area, the sector authorities register the dead, but no one asked about the women or what their problems were." Perpetue from Taba commune had a more direct exchange with an inspector:

> I went to report what happened to me to the local authorities in Taba in March 1996. I spoke with the judicial police inspector and told him that I knew the names of some of the men who had raped me. He told me that rape was not a reason to accuse a person and that there are no arguments to bring those sorts of

---

[151]Human Rights Watch/FIDH interview, prosecutor, April 3, 1996.

[152]Human Rights Watch/FIDH interview, Gerald Gahima, Deputy Minister of Justice, Kigali, April 4, 1996.

[153]Human Rights Watch/FIDH interview, Shyanda commune, Butare prefecture April 2, 1996.

killed and if I saw it myself. I was crying. It was not worth it to
say that she was raped.[157]

In other cases, women have not reported perpetrators of their rapes because they
have no confidence in the justice system and because they fear reprisals. In some
cases, the perpetrators continue to live nearby, and even if they have been
imprisoned, the women fear they will find a way to take retribution. Goretti, a rape
survivor, said, "I do not think it's worthwhile to accuse my attackers. If they are
released from prison, I am afraid that they will follow me and harm me more."[158]

The issue of justice for rape survivors is extremely important. After
several months of debate, on August 9, 1996, the National Assembly passed
legislation which will govern the prosecution of crimes of genocide and crimes
against humanity in Rwanda, including rape (See Rape as a Crime Under Rwandan
Law). The prosecution and punishment of perpetrators of rape will acknowledge
the injustice committed against the rape survivors, and help to remove the stigma
of rape by recognizing that rape is a crime. However, given the problems within
the judicial system, the possibility of reduced sentences and the reluctance of
women to come forward because of stigma and fear, the likelihood of justice for
Rwandan rape survivors remains distant. Impunity for the perpetrators of rape will
perpetuate the silence surrounding this issue and send a message to Rwandan
women that the sexual violence against them was not a crime.

The International Criminal Tribunal

Since 1990, the international community has adopted a more
institutionalized response to atrocities committed in conflict than in the past. In
particular, two International Criminal Tribunals have been created by the U.N.
Security Council to hold perpetrators of the violence accountable in an
international procedure in the former Yugoslavia and in Rwanda.[159] The precursors

---

[157]Human Rights Watch/FIDH interview, Rusatira commune, Butare prefecture,
March 24, 1996.

[158]Human Rights Watch/FIDH interview, Rusatira commune, Butare prefecture,
March 23, 1996.

[159]In the case of Yugoslavia, the Security Council established first a commission
of experts pursuant to resolution 780(1992) and then the International Criminal Tribunal for
the Prosecution of Persons Responsible for Serious Violations of International Humanitarian
Law Committed in the Territory of the Former Yugoslavia since 1991. The Commission

to such Tribunals were the International Military Tribunal at Nuremberg and the International Military Tribunal for the Far East (the Tokyo Tribunal). In 1994, a commission of experts was established in the context of the genocide in Rwanda pursuant to Security Council resolution 935(1994) to examine and analyze grave violations of international law in Rwanda.

The International Criminal Tribunal for Rwanda was created by the United Nations Security Council Resolution 955 of November 8, 1994. The resolution stipulated that the Tribunal would be vested with the authority to prosecute persons responsible for serious violations of international humanitarian law committed in Rwanda and by Rwandan citizens responsible for such violations committed in the territory of neighboring states between January 1, 1994 and December 31, 1994. Arusha, Tanzania was declared the seat of the Tribunal by resolution S/1995/148 of February 21, 1995. The Tribunal began its work on June 26, 1995, which was the day of the first plenary session of its eleven judges in The Hague, Netherlands.[160] The Tribunal is vested with the authority to prosecute persons who

---

of Experts conducted investigations into violations of international humanitarian law against persons, including extrajudicial executions, torture and other violations of international humanitarian law, particularly in detention camps. Special emphasis was given in these investigations to allegations of rape and sexual assault. The report of the Secretary-General pursuant to para. 2 of Security Council resolution 808(1993), discussing the competence of the International Criminal Tribunal for the former Yugoslavia, refers to crimes against humanity as being inhumane acts of a very serious nature, such as willful killing, torture, or rape, committed as part of a widespread or systematic attack against any civilian population on national, political, ethnic, racial or religious grounds, and states that "in the conflict in the territory of the former Yugoslavia, such inhuman acts have taken the form of so-called ethnic cleansing and widespread and systematic rape and other forms of sexual assault, including forced prostitution." "Report of the Secretary-General pursuant to paragraph 2 of the Security Council resolution 808" (1993)(S/25704), para.48 as quoted in the Preliminary report submitted by the Special Rapporteur on Violence against Women, its Causes and Consequences, p. 64-65.

---

[160]The trial chamber judges are: Navanethem Pillay (South Africa); Lennart Aspegren (Sweden); Laity Kama (Senegal); Tafazzal Hossain Khan (Bangladesh); Yakov A. Ostrovsky (Russia) and William H. Cecal (Tanzania). The Appeals Chamber consists of Georges Abi-Saab (Egypt); Antonio Cassese (Italy); Jules Deschênes (Canada); Haopei Li (China); and Ninian Stephen (Australia). The Deputy Prosecutor is Judge Honoré Rakotomanana (Madagascar). Judge Navanethem Pillay is the only woman on this team. Starting in the fall of 1996, the Chief Prosecutor for both Tribunals will be Judge Louise Arbour, a Canadian. The Tribunal for the Former Yugoslavia currently has two female judges: Gabrielle Kirk McDonald (United States), and Elizabeth Odio-Benito (Costa Rica).

committed genocide, crimes against humanity, and violations of Common Article 3 of the Geneva Conventions and of the Additional Protocol II of the Geneva Conventions which govern internal armed conflicts. Genocide includes acts committed with the intent to destroy, in whole or in part, a national, ethnic, racial or religious group.

Rape is clearly a prosecutable crime under the mandate of the International Criminal Tribunal for Rwanda. It is explicitly identified as one of the crimes against humanity (along with murder, extermination, enslavement, deportation, imprisonment, torture, persecutions on political, racial and religious grounds and other inhumane acts).[161] The Statute also specifies rape to be a violation of Article 3 common to the Geneva Conventions and of Additional Protocol II.[162] Rape can also be a form of torture under international law as well as an act of genocide.[163] At this time, the International Criminal Tribunal for Rwanda is undertaking its investigation and compiling evidence to bring indictments against those accused of organizing the genocide. Twenty-one persons have been indicted, in thirteen indictments, although only nine names have been made public; the remaining names have not been disclosed, pending arrest. Three of those indicted are in custody in Arusha;[164] four are in Cameroon;[165] one is in Belgium;[166] one is

---

[161]Security Council Resolution 955 (1994), establishing the International Tribunal for Rwanda, Annex, Article 3.

[162]Ibid. Annex, Article 4.

[163]See section on "International and National Legal Protections Against Gender-Based Violence."

[164]The three in custody in Arusha are: Georges Anderson Nderubumwe Rutaganda, Jean Paul Akayesu, and Clement Kayishema. Their initial hearings were held in Arusha on May 30 and 31, 1996. They pleaded not guilty.

[165]The four in detention in Cameroon are: Ferdinand Nahimana, Anatole Nsengiyumva, Theoneste Bagosora, and André Ntajerura. On August 9, Bagosora and Ntajerura were indicted, and on August 10, Judge Lennart Aspergren confirmed the indictments and delivered warrants of arrest. Their transfer to Arusha will take place as soon as the President of Cameroon makes the authorization.

[166]The one in detention in Belgium is Joseph Kanyabashi.

in Switzerland.[167] However, at this writing, the court itself has not begun to hear the cases. The twenty-one have been indicted on various counts of genocide, crimes against humanity, violations of Article 3 of the Geneva Conventions, and violations of additional Protocol 2.

Unfortunately, the manner in which the International Criminal Tribunal for Rwanda has been conducting its investigations strongly suggests that unless it takes active steps, it may fail to mount even one rape prosecution. The Tribunal has been using methodology and investigative procedures that preclude it from effectively obtaining rape testimonies in Rwanda. Little has been done to competently include gender-based violence at the investigative stage. In a positive development, in July 1996, a Sexual Assault Committee was created within the Tribunal. The committee is comprised of representatives from each investigative team and will address strategic, legal and methodological questions confronting the investigations.

The Rwanda Tribunal has also faced serious resource, staffing and logistical constraints, since the international community did not give the Tribunal the funding necessary to effectively carry out the important work that it was established to do. Although in June 1996 the Tribunal finally received commitments for a budget of U.S. $35 million, which would allow it to hire approximately 100 investigators, in 1995 the budget was approximately U.S. $16.9 million, of which only U.S. $1.6 million was spent. As of August 1996, there were still only some thirty investigators who were responsible for collecting a massive amount of evidence. Of those, four were women. With regard to gender-based crimes, the Tribunal's problems are all magnified. If the Tribunal does not take immediate steps to address these problems and conduct effective investigations to collect the testimonies of rape victims, by the time cases are brought before the Tribunal judges it will be too late to include rape charges.

The lack of investigation of rape, however, is due to problems largely unrelated to resources. First, the lack of investigation of rape is a result of a lack of political will on the part of those responsible for leading the investigations. There is a widespread perception among the Tribunal investigators that rape is somehow a "lesser" or "incidental" crime not worth investigating. There is also the mistaken perception that, because the rapes against Rwandan women do not mirror the exact experience of rape victims in Yugoslavia, which involved issues such as forced impregnation, the Rwanda Tribunal need not spend time investigating the Rwandan rapes.

---

[167]The one in detention in Switzerland is Alfred Musema.

Second, there is the mistaken assertion by staff members of the Tribunal that they do not need to devote scarce resources to investigating rape because Rwandan women will not come forward to talk. The Deputy Prosecutor of the Rwandan Tribunal told Human Rights Watch/FIDH that the reason they have not collected rape testimonies is because "African women don't want to talk about rape . . . We haven't received any real complaints. It's rare in investigations that women refer to rape."[168] As this report indicates, if interviews are conducted in conditions of safety and privacy, and if Rwandan women believe that telling their testimony will help bring about justice, they will talk.

Third, even where Tribunal investigators do try to document rape, they are using interviewing techniques that are poorly designed to gain the confidence of the women, elicit rape testimonies and ensure protection from retaliation. In the Rwandan context, it is essential that women are approached through an interlocutor whom they trust, such as someone from the community or a women's organization with whom they are familiar. Interviews must be conducted in privacy and without a large group of people. Rwandan women have also indicated that they are more comfortable telling their testimonies to women investigators, and when necessary with women interpreters, in large part because of the stigma attached to rape. In some areas, women even specified that the woman translator had to be another genocide survivor and not a returnee, because of the tension between the survivors and returnees.

The Tribunal has been conducting its investigations without regard to these factors, and as a result, has not documented rape testimonies. Tribunal interviews are always conducted in pairs, often with a Kinyarwanda interpreter present. Most of the investigators and interpreters are male. Although the guidelines given to investigators contain a reminder to ask about rape, where relevant, there is no further guidance to investigators on how to approach the issue in a manner that will allow women to speak. The Tribunal investigators have also been reluctant to work with local women's organizations to identify women victims of rape on the grounds that it might compromise their perceived impartiality.

Most Rwandan women interviewed by Human Rights Watch/FIDH had not heard of the International Criminal Tribunal, although some knew of its existence from the radio. None, however, had spoken to a Tribunal investigator. Those who had heard of the Tribunal urged that the Tribunal do something to prosecute rape. For these rape victims, an International Criminal Tribunal may be their only opportunity to see the crimes against them denounced, to see both the

---

[168] Human Rights Watch/FIDH interview, Judge Honoré Rakotomanana, deputy prosecutor, International Criminal Tribunal, Kigali, March 27, 1996.

perpetrators of such abuse and the commanders who allowed and participated in rape and other abuses prosecuted, and to seek a remedy for the assaults they have suffered. Clementine, a rape survivor said, "I have heard of the International Criminal Tribunal and I hope that they can do something, because we don't want our children to see what we have seen."[169]

Victim and Witness Protection

If women agree to testify, effective protection for rape victims must also be guaranteed by the Tribunal. Many women fear reprisals if they testify. These fears are not unwarranted. Witnesses and survivors of the genocide continue to be killed in the country and abroad. For other women, the stigma of rape will deter them from coming forward if they cannot be assured that their privacy will be protected. Unless the Tribunal takes steps to ensure that adequate privacy and security is provided to rape survivors who agree to testify, it is unlikely that women will agree to testify. Without such measures, there is also a likelihood that the effort to bring the perpetrators to justice through the Tribunal could further contribute to the trauma already experienced by the women.

The Rules of Procedure and Evidence of the International Criminal Tribunal for Rwanda does address the need for witness protection. Rule 34 allows for the creation of a Victims and Witnesses Unit:

> (a)   There shall be set up under the authority of the Registrar a Victims and Witnesses Unit consisting of qualified staff to:
>
> > (i)   recommend protective measures for victims and witnesses in accordance with Article 21 of the Statute; and
> >
> > (ii)   provide counseling and support for them, in particular in cases of rape and sexual assault.
>
> (b)   Due consideration shall be given, in the appointment of staff, to the employment of qualified women.[170]

---

[169]Human Rights Watch/FIDH interview, Shyanda commune, Butare prefecture, March 26, 1996.

[170]The Rules of Procedure and Evidence of the International Tribunal for Rwanda/3, Rev. 1, June 29, 1995, Rule 34 as quoted in Coordination of Women's Advocacy, "Mission on Gender-Based War Crimes Against Women and Girls During the Genocide in Rwanda: Summary of Findings and Recommendations," Geneva, July 1995,

Rule 69 also deals with the protection of women. This rule relates to the non-disclosure of the identity of a victim or witness who may be in danger until s/he is brought under the protection of the Tribunal and also provides for the disclosure of the name of a victim or witness "in sufficient time" for the adequate preparation of defense.

The Witnesses Unit was established under the registrar's office in Arusha in July 1996, but at this writing, it is not yet operative. Given that trials are expected to begin in late September or October 1996, the Tribunal must immediately address the need to establish mechanisms for protecting victims and witnesses.

The Witness Protection Unit is supposed to rely on national governments to protect individuals identified by the Tribunal, since the Unit does not have its own protection force. In principle, this also would require the governments in the region—including Zaire and Kenya, which have already refused to cooperate with the Tribunal's investigations—to be responsible for protecting certain individuals whose security is deemed at risk. However, the vast majority of women involved are in Rwanda, and therefore protection arrangements must be made with the Rwandan government to ensure the security of those identified by the Tribunal.

Support services must also be provided to victims and witnesses, including legal counseling to prepare them for giving testimony; trauma counseling, especially for those who suffered sexual abuse; medical attention; transport for family or other victims to accompany victims or witnesses to Arusha; and relocation of victims, witnesses, and their families, if they so desire.

The United Nations Human Rights Operation

There is a United Nations Human Rights Field Operation (HRFOR) currently in Rwanda. The mandate of the Human Rights Operation includes the following responsibilities (italics added):

(a)	*To carry out investigations into violations of human rights and humanitarian law,* including possible acts of genocide, in accordance with directives given by the Special Rapporteur on the situation of human rights in Rwanda and the Commission of Experts . . .;

(b)	*To monitor the ongoing human rights situation, and through their presence help redress existing problems*

p. 13.

> *and prevent possible human rights violations from*
> *occurring;*

(c)   To cooperate with other international agencies in
          charge of re-establishing confidence and thus facilitate
          the return of refugees and displaced persons and the
          rebuilding of civic society;

(d)   *To implement programmes of technical cooperation in*
          the field of human rights, particularly in the area of the
          administration of justice; and

(e)   To report to the High Commissioner who will make
          information available to the Special Rapporteur on the
          situation of human rights in Rwanda and the
          Commission of Experts . . .[171]

Under its mandate, there are a number of areas in which the Human Rights
Field Operation can address gender-specific human rights abuses, including to
investigate and document reports of sexual violence by state actors and to monitor
justice problems that women are currently facing when they attempt to bring
charges of rape to the Rwandan judiciary. The Human Rights Operation should
apply its monitoring and advisory role to ensuring the well-being of women who
are already victims of genocide, and require assistance in order to enjoy equal
protection under the law, including the non-discriminatory respect of their property
and inheritance rights. At the moment, however, the Human Rights Operation has
no thematic focus to address current human rights problems facing women.

The International Response
          Since July 1994, the international community has spent approximately
U.S. $2.5 billion on the Rwandan refugee camps in Zaire and Tanzania, while
devoting about U.S. $572 million to programs in Rwanda itself.[172]   This
overwhelming focus on the refugees, many of whom participated in the genocide,

---

[171]Agreement Between the United Nations and the Government of Rwanda on the
Status of the Human Rights Mission in Rwanda (undated), p. 3.

[172]In the June 1996 Rwanda Roundtable held in Geneva, U.S. $617 million was
pledged for 1997-1998.

has caused considerable resentment within Rwanda, both on the part of the Rwandan government and on the part of ordinary Rwandans.

Within the overall aid program to Rwanda, a fairly small amount is targeted for gender-related issues, ranging from assistance for women in terms of housing, credit and income-generating activities to health care and trauma counseling. Despite a significant level of aid going to the Rwandan judiciary, there are currently no programs designed to enhance the capacity of Rwandan police or judicial police inspectors to investigate gender-related crimes, including rape and sexual violence during the genocide and current abuses against women. Some assistance is being provided for reform of discriminatory aspects of the legal code, including inheritance law, although much more is needed in order to move that process forward.

The United Nations

Most donors are providing assistance to Rwanda through either United Nations agencies or international nongovernmental organizations. Donor assistance channeled through the United Nations Development Program (UNDP) since the beginning of the crisis amounts to almost U.S. $53 million. This assistance funded projects for the justice sector, governmental capacity building, refugees and internally displaced persons. UNDP considers assistance to women to be covered under projects for vulnerable groups, such as resettlement and housing. These projects are supported by funding from Japan (U.S. $2 million) and the Netherlands (U.S. $2,978,000).[173]

As of May 1996, UNDP had approved eight projects in the justice sector, amounting to U.S. $12.7 million. The projects include training of public prosecutors, posting of foreign legal advisors to assist with the genocide prosecutions, providing transportation and other equipment to criminal police inspectors, and construction of detention facilities. None of these projects target gender-based issues. Contributions to these programs have come from the Netherlands, the United Kingdom, Sweden, the United States, Switzerland, Japan, Finland, Spain and Ireland.

The United Nations Development Fund for Women (UNIFEM) is funding programs for women in selected displaced persons camps and returnee women's groups in Rwanda. Through its African Women in Crisis initiative, UNIFEM focuses on reproductive health, trauma management, and quality of life improvement (including skills training and income generation projects) for women

---

[173]Facsimile from Ms. Olubanke King-Akerele, Chief, Division I, UNDP Regional Bureau for Africa, to Janet Fleischman, Human Rights Watch/Africa, August 1, 1996.

and girls in Rwanda. The program is funded at U.S. $885,000, which includes: the reproductive health and trauma management project, U.S. $210,000; the women income generation project, U.S. $175,000; and supplies and logistics, U.S. $500,000. In 1994, the Swedish government contributed U.S. $135,000 to the project. In 1995, the government of Luxembourg contributed U.S. $210,000. In addition, UNDP recently approved a U.S. $1 million Japanese Trust Fund project to promote shelter for widows and women's economic empowerment, to be executed by the Ministry of Women and managed by UNIFEM.[174]

The United Nations Children's Fund (UNICEF) has instituted a program with the Ministry of Justice for the protection of children in conflict with the law, which also includes programs for women in detention, such as advocacy and support for pregnant women and women in prison with their children; reinforcing the Ministry of Justice's Inspection Unit for monitoring the detention conditions in prisons and municipal jails for women and children; support to the Gendarmerie for the creation of specialized teams of judicial police officers in each prefecture who will be trained in arrest procedures, detention, and general treatment of women and children.

The United States

Like other donors, the U. S. has given the bulk of its assistance to the refugee camps: out of a total of U.S. $750 million for humanitarian assistance in the Great Lakes since 1994, U.S. $408 million has been for the camps; U.S. $243 million for Rwanda; and U.S. $100 million for Burundi.[175] The figures for disaster assistance have also diminished considerably since the start of the crisis, with the U.S. providing U.S. $31 million in the second half of 1994, falling to U.S. $25 million in 1995, and finally U.S. $2 million in 1996.

Current U.S. assistance is divided between two programs: democracy and governance, which includes administration of justice, and aid to the displaced, including health, food security, family reunification and aid to orphans. Assistance to women falls into the latter category. The U.S. government has recognized the importance of providing assistance to Rwandan women, many of whom are widows and, for the first time, heads of households. In a speech at the Rwanda

---

[174]Facsimile from Laketch Dirasse, Senior Manager, UNIFEM/AFWIC, to Janet Fleischman, Human Rights Watch/Africa, August 27, 1996.

[175]U.S. Agency for International Development, "Summary: USG Humanitarian Assistance for Burundi, Rwanda, and the Rwanda Regional Crisis, FYs 1994, 1995, and 1996."

Roundtable on June 20-21, 1996, Richard McCall, Chief of Staff for the U.S. Agency for International Development (AID), identified assistance to women as a U.S. objective:

> Continued emphasis should be given to credit schemes that provide funds for women who work together in collaborative groups to identify and address their family and community income needs. The majority of such on-going projects carried out by women's associations or groups are made up of widows or women who are caring for an average of two to four foster children in addition to their own. It is manifest that the women of Rwanda are key agents of change on the local level during this important transitional phase.[176]

To this end, the State Department's Office of Transition Initiatives (OTI) and AID are funding a project called Women in Transition initiative, which is designed as a partnership between the Ministry of Family and Women and AID to assist women, particularly widows and those heading households, in rebuilding their lives. In FY 1995, OTI provided U.S. $1 million, and AID is expected to provide an additional U.S. $750,000 in 1996 (with FY 1995 funds). The priority areas for funding are programs dealing with shelter and credit, followed by agriculture, women's rights education, literacy, community mobilization, cooperative enterprises, and capacity building for structures that support women at the central and communal level.

The U.S. government is also providing assistance to the justice system. In the fiscal year 1995, the U.S. provided U.S. $4.3 million to the Rwandan judicial system: U.S. $275,000 for a five-day conference on Genocide, Impunity and Accountability in Rwanda in November 1995;[177] U.S. $139,000 for a Justice Advisor to work with the Rwandan government; U.S. $500,000 to the International Rescue Committee for rehabilitation of justice buildings; U.S. $1.2 million for

---

[176]Mr. Richard McCall, Chief of Staff of U.S. Agency for International Development, "U.S. Statement," Rwanda Roundtable, Geneva, June 20-21, 1996.

[177]The conference recommended a fast track for genocide cases, a compensation fund for victims, and an official memorial commission. AID considers its biggest contribution to the justice system to be the policy debate and draft legislation developed from the genocide conference.

police training, for both the gendarmerie and communal police;[178] U.S. $100,000 for bilingual legal training to Butare University;[179] U.S. $1 million for identity cards, and U.S. $40,000 for English summary translations of Rwandan laws.

The U.S. provided an additional U.S. $1.2 million for the U.N. Human Rights Field Operation in 1995 and U.S. $3 million to the International Tribunal in 1995, with U.S. $500,000 in FY 1996.

It is commendable that the U.S. has provided assistance to women in general through the Women in Transition Initiative, but it should also ensure that some of its assistance to the judicial system, to the U.N. Human Rights Office, and to the International Tribunal be used to assist in bringing to justice the perpetrators of rape and those guilty of other abuses against women.

The European Union (EU)

EU assistance to Rwanda since 1994 totals ECU 535.071.646 (U.S. $417 million). This includes aid and technical assistance for the reconstruction of the judiciary and for women in development, with a component for revision of the legal codes and judicial assistance for women. Most of the assistance is humanitarian and is channeled through European Community Humanitarian Office (ECHO), amounting to ECU 355.430.000 (U.S. $277 million).

The EU has also provided approximately ECU 1,500,000 (U.S. $1,170,000) for the International Tribunal. For the U.N. Human Rights Field Operation, the EU provided ECU 1,059,069 (U.S. $826,000) in 1995 and ECU 5,479,992 (U.S. $4,275,000) in 1996.[180]

---

[178]International Criminal Investigative Training Assistance Program (ICITAP) began operating in Rwanda in May 1996. In April, senior communal police and gendarmerie officers went on a two-week tour of the U.S. for exposure to U.S. models of policing.

[179]In May 1996, the University of Quebec sent law instructors to Butare University to teach civil law and develop a curriculum in English. Since English is now an official language in Rwanda and many government officials do not speak French, this program is an effort to encourage English-speakers to participate in the French-based legal system.

[180]Letter from B. Collingwood, VIII/E/2, G12-04/112, European Commission, Directorate for General Development, East and Southern Africa, to Lotte Leicht, Human Rights Watch Brussels Director, July 31, 1996.

The Netherlands

In 1995 and 1996, the Netherlands government provided approximately U.S. $101.7 million for relief and reconstruction in Rwanda and the Great Lakes region.[181] For Rwanda, this included U.S. $16 million for the UNDP Trust Fund, U.S. $13.5 million for the justice system, U.S. $4.2 for prisons and police, U.S. $19 million for resettlement for IDPs and refugees, and U.S. $11.82 for bilateral projects. The justice program included training for magistrates and judicial police inspectors, as well as sending twenty-one experts to the International Tribunal for Rwanda. The prisons/police program included support for the UNDP training for communal police. Training those working on justice issues at the national and international level about gender-based crimes against women should be made a component of these programs.

The Netherlands is also providing funding for education programs, an advisory expert for the Ministry of Health, and the Gender Development Fund of the Ministry of Women and Family. The Dutch government should ensure that their overall program address the special needs of Rwanda's women.

---

[181]"Netherlands Assistance to the Great Lakes Region in 1995 and 1996," provided to Human Rights Watch/Africa by the Dutch Foreign Ministry, August 1, 1996.